PIANO
The

JANE CAMPION

BLOOMSBURY

First published in Great Britain 1993

Copyright © 1992 by Jan Chapman Productions Pty Ltd

The moral right of the author has been asserted

Bloomsbury Publishing Ltd, 2 Soho Square, London W1V 5DE

A CIP catalogue record for this book is available from the British Library

ISBN 0 7475 1685 5

10 9 8 7 6 5 4 3 2

Typeset by Hewer Text Composition Services, Edinburgh
Designed by Penny Edwards
Printed in Great Britain by St Edmundsbury Press, Suffolk

Photographs by Grant Matthews and Polly Walker
Script editor Billy Mackinnon
Producer Jan Chapman

CONTENTS

I think that the romantic impulse is in all of us and that sometimes we live it for a short time, but it's not part of a sensible way of living. It's a heroic path and it generally ends dangerously. I treasure it in the sense that I believe it's a path of great courage. It can also be the path of the foolhardy and the compulsive.

Jane Campion

For Edith

THE PIANO

1. ADA (V.O. Scenes 2–7).

> The voice you hear is not my speaking voice,
> but my mind's voice.

> I have not spoken since I was six years old. No
> one knows why, not even me. My father says it
> is a dark talent and the day I take it into my
> head to stop breathing will be my last.

> Today he married me to a man I've not yet met.
> Soon my daughter and I shall join him in his
> own country. My husband said my muteness
> does not bother him. He writes and hark this:
> God loves dumb creatures, so why not he!

> Were good he had God's patience for silence
> affects everyone in the end. The strange thing is
> I don't think myself silent, that is, because of
> my piano. I shall miss it on the journey.

2. EXT. SCOTTISH FIELD NEAR HOUSE. DAY.
*A woman in a dark crêpe Victorian dress sits leaning
against a tree; her hands cover her face, around her neck
she wears a writing pad. She crosses a field with large bare
trees; in the far background stands a three-storey stone
house.*

3. INT. SCOTTISH HOUSE CORRIDOR. DAY.
A small girl roller skates down a dimly lit corridor. A parlour maid looks down the hall where the girl has disappeared.

4. INT. SCOTTISH HOUSE DRAWING ROOM. DAY.
Three men wearing long grey aprons are fitting the packing for a piano. On one of the men's arms is a tattoo of a whale in a wild sea.

5. EXT. SCOTTISH HOUSE GROUNDS. DAY.
The girl wearing her skates sits on a small black pony. An old man is pulling it, but it won't move. (In the background, another aspect of the grey stone house.)

6. INT. SCOTTISH HOUSE, FLORA'S BEDROOM. NIGHT.
The woman lifts back the sheets from the bottom of the sleeping girl's bed. She is still wearing her skates. The woman cuts through the laces and removes the boots. One disembodied skate rolls across the room.

7. INT. SCOTTISH HOUSE DRAWING ROOM. NIGHT.
The woman stands at a window lit by moonlight. Her skin appears luminescently white. She touches the wooden window frame, the curtain, the objects on the window sill, her mind abstracted, her hands unconsciously performing a farewell. Turning from the window she moves to a square piano crowded by packing boxes. In the dim light she begins to play strongly. Her face strains, she is utterly involved, unaware of her own strange guttural sounds that form an eerie accompaniment to the music.

An old maid in night-dress looks in. Abruptly the woman stops playing. The emotion leaves her face, it whitens and seems solid like a wall.

10

CUT TO BLACK

8. EXT. UNDERWATER BEACH. DAY.

Underwater a long boat passes overhead, its oars breaking the surface.

9. EXT. BEACH. DAY.

Amidst a riotous sea a woman, ADA, *is carried to shore on the shoulders of five seamen. Her large Victorian skirt spreads across the men's arms and backs, on her head a black bonnet, around her neck her pad and pen. We should be forgiven if this woman seems a sacrificial offering as the bay they carry her to is completely uninhabited. A black sand backs on to an endless rise of dense native bush.*

The breakers are chaotic, the men strain to keep their footing, calling to each other.

SEAMEN: Hold still, you smutt! Blast the boat! Look up! Look up! Lay to! Lay to! Up with it, you buggerers, hold hard! Damn me, won't you hold?! [Etc.]

Two of the men are black, all are battered, tattooed and tough, some are drunk.

Behind the woman is her daughter, a girl of 10 in Scottish dress. She too is carried on the shoulders of seamen.

ADA *is placed on the sand. She looks down at her feet sinking into the wet sand, then up at the huge confusion of fern and bush in front of her. The sound of the sea behind is thunderous.*

Several of the seamen have formed a group and are pissing on the sand.

Her daughter is on all fours evidently being sick. But

12

ADA's *attention is diverted to the seamen who are staggering through the waves with a huge piano-shaped box. They put it down as soon as they get to shore but* ADA *makes gestures that they must immediately bring it to higher, safer, ground. The piano placed to her satisfaction she hovers near it, one hand in constant touch of it while her daughter grips her free hand.*

10. EXT. BEACH. DAY.
TWO SEAMEN *finish carrying the last crate to shore.*[1]
Trunks and boxes including an open crate with hens are scattered carelessly along the shore.

The SEAMEN *gather together. After a discussion in which they look between* ADA *and her child and their coaster out on the sea, one of the men approaches. Behind him the other men keep their eyes out to sea or down on the sand. They don't want to be involved. The sight of the women alone on this beach is too hopeless.*

SEAMAN: It's a little rough out there. Could be they can't get through to you in this weather. Maybe they'll come over land.
ADA *nods.*
SEAMAN: Have you things for shelter?
ADA *nods.*
SEAMAN: What things have you?
ADA *signs to her daughter. The little girl speaks clearly and loudly without emotion.*
FLORA: She says 'thank you'.
Puzzled, the man walks off, then turns and comes back.
SEAMAN: Does your mother prefer to come on with us to Nelson?

[1] See notes, p. 125.

ADA *signs vigorously to* FLORA.

FLORA: She says, No. She says she'd rather be boiled alive by natives than get back in your tub.

SEAMAN: (*Stunned.*) You be damn fortuned I don't smack your puppy gob, missy. Damn lucky.

11. EXT. BEACH. DAY.

FLORA *watches the seamen down at the water's edge. She watches as their boat gets smaller and smaller. Then, suddenly aware of herself alone and distant, from both the boat and her mother, she runs frantically up the beach to her mother. The two women are but tiny dots on the shore and the view continues back and back over a vast, endless expanse of dense native bush.*

12. EXT. BEACH. DAY.

ADA *is sheltering anxiously behind the crated piano.* FLORA *is asleep at her feet, a half-eaten biscuit in her hand.* ADA *has found a gap through the crate so that she might lift the lid and play a few notes.*[2] *The sweetness and comfort of the piano seem only to exaggerate their isolation and hopelessness.*

Suddenly a rush of sea water shoots straight under the raised crate of the piano, wetting her shoes. ADA *stands, pushing* FLORA *on to her feet. She is aghast to see the tide has crept in completely unnoticed.*

They watch three of their boxes float out to sea. One of the hens has escaped the crate and is bobbing up and down in the waves.

13. EXT. BEACH. LATE AFTERNOON.

It is evening. A grey-green light. ADA *and* FLORA *run out*

[2] See notes, p. 125.

along the huge expanse of sand. The tide is low now and the sand looks smooth and slippery like a seal's back. The two women stop and look up and down the beach. Still no one is coming.

14. EXT. BEACH. DUSK.
There is just a pink streak left in the sky. ADA *and* FLORA *shelter inside their makeshift tent, a hooped petticoat secured at the edges with stones. Inside the tent a candle lights up their conversation.*

*   ADA *is hand-signalling a story to* FLORA *who lies back watching, nervous and afraid.* ADA's *whole self is involved in the 'telling'; her face is alight with expression, now tender, now sad, now humorous, now soft, while her hands and fingers are deft and precise. From outside it is an odd shadow-play.*

FLORA (*Hand-signalling.*): Mother . . . I'm thinking.
ADA *pauses.*
FLORA (*Speaking.*): I'm not going to call him Papa, I'm not going to call HIM anything. I'm not even going to look at HIM.

15. EXT. BUSH ON WAY TO BEACH. DAY.
Through a dense bush walk a party of fourteen MAORI MEN *and* WOMEN *and two* EUROPEAN MEN. *The wetness, closeness and darkness of the bush is such that the air seems green, as at the bottom of a deep sea. Two of the* MAORIS *share one pair of shoes and all of them are clothed in a mixture of native and European costume. Of the Europeans one is small and has a shy manner. He has a half-completed Maori tattoo across his cheeks. The other is a similar age, about 45, and wears a suit, muddy and out of place here in the bush. He staggers, spurts forward, then slows to a stop.*

17

*His hair and face are wet and his skin reflects the green
foliage.* BAINES, *the younger man, turns and slows.*
BAINES: Are we stopping? . . . Do you want to stop?
The MAORI *voices and laughter are becoming fainter.*[3]
BAINES *watches, torn between his concern for* STEWART
and the split in their party.

BAINES: Shall we stop?
Unable to get an answer, BAINES *runs after the* MAORIS.
BAINES: *Tai hoa! Me tatari tatou . . . me tutatou i konei.*
    [*Subtitled*: Wait! We are stopping . . . we're stopping.]
STEWART *takes out a comb and drags it dazed and
zombie-like through his wet hair. Inside the darkness of his
pocket, he turns over and over a small, worn-edged
photograph: a smudge of green light allows us to see*
ADA's *tumbling face. Taking it in the heel of his hand he
secretly looks at it. Just as the party returns and settles he
strides on ahead, possessed and determined.*
STEWART: We must get on.
The MAORIS *look at* BAINES, *bewildered.*
TAME: *Aue tepatupaiarehe!*
    [*Subtitled*: The fairy people, what can you expect?]

16. EXT. BEACH. EARLY MORNING.
*It is early morning. The sea is calmer and the tide is again
low. The party of two* EUROPEANS *and fourteen* MAORI
MEN *and* WOMEN *comes out on to the beach. About half
the* MAORI *party heads straight for the shoreline where an
older woman loudly organizes a* pipi *collection. All sorts
of containers are used, from flax baskets to shirts with
knots in their arms. The rest follow* STEWART *and* BAINES

[3] See notes, p. 125.

over to the boxes. STEWART *automatically re-combs his hair, patting it against his forehead, where it sticks in a raked pattern. On his head he carefully places a formal top hat, oddly clean compared to his mud-splattered suit. The party stops short of the petticoats where a tell-tale foot reveals its occupants.*

STEWART: Miss McGrath, Alisdair Stewart. You'll have to wake yourself. I've got men here to carry your things.

ADA *and* FLORA *struggle up to find themselves confronted by a group of men and women. The* MAORIS *stare curiously and comment on the women:*

Aue he anahera enei?

[*Subtitled*: Are they angels? They look like angels.]

A man points at FLORA'*s feet and gestures as if holding one of the little shoes in his hand:*

Te monohi hoki!

[*Subtitled*: So small!]

FLORA *is struck by shyness and hides under her mother's skirt.* ADA *cannot look straight at* STEWART *and* STEWART *also cannot look at her.*

STEWART: I see you have a good many boxes, I'd like to know what is in each.

As ADA *does not move,* STEWART *is puzzled.*

STEWART: CAN – YOU – HEAR – ME?

ADA *nods and looks up coldly, insulted by his slow, loud, speaking.*

STEWART: Well that is good, yes, that is good, good.

STEWART, *smiling, searches* ADA'*s face for some sign of comprehension but is unnerved by her lack of response. He stops smiling, and, patting his hair, walks to the closest box. Several of the* MAORI *party follow behind* STEWART *while one of them closely and particularly mimics him.*

STEWART: What's in here?

ADA *points to the writing already on the box saying*
'Crockery and Pots'.

STEWART: Ohh, yes, so it is, written there, crockery . . .
   And this one?

ADA *writes 'bedclothes and linen' on the pad around her*
neck. While she writes he takes the opportunity to
scrutinize her.

STEWART: You're small. I never thought you'd be small.
He walks to another chest.

STEWART: What's here?

She writes 'clothes'. The MAORI *mimic also pretends to*
write.

   Finally he comes to the piano box. He lifts a corner
experimentally.

STEWART: What's in here then, lead?

FLORA (*Gravely.*): It's my mother's piano.

STEWART: A piano?

The MAORIS *touch the exposed legs of the piano.*

   STEWART *speaks to the other European man,* BAINES.

STEWART: Tell them to carry in pairs. Those three and
   those two the black and the red, then the suitcases.

STEWART *holds* BAINES *back a moment.*

STEWART: What do you think?

STEWART *nods towards* ADA. BAINES *thinks a moment*
then turns towards ADA *too.*

BAINES: She looks tired.

STEWART: She's stunted, that's one thing.

BAINES *walks over to* HONE, *a big man and the* MAORI
leader; he stands tall with a great sense of his own
importance (mana).

BAINES: *Anei nga pouaka – ko era e toro. Me era e raa.*
   [*Subtitled*: Here are the boxes, those three and those
   two.]

22

HONE: *E Hoa!*

HONE *takes an aggressive fighting posture towards* BAINES, *insulted that* BAINES *should suggest he might carry anything.* HONE *does no carrying, he is the boss. With great dignity* HONE *retreats, too injured to help. Other* MAORIS *come up and* BAINES *assigns them boxes.* ADA *gets worried, the piano is being left alone. She writes on her pad, 'THE PIANO?' She shows* STEWART.

STEWART: Oh no, it can't come now.

FLORA: It must come.

STEWART *looks at* FLORA.

FLORA: . . . she wants it to come.

STEWART: Yes, and so do I, but there are too few of us here to carry it. TOO – HEAVY.

ADA *writes 'I NEED THE PIANO'. Her* MAORI *mimic copies her.*

STEWART: Do you mean you don't want your kitchenware or your clothes? Is that what you mean?

ADA *signs to* FLORA.

FLORA: We can't leave the piano.

STEWART: Let us not discuss this further. I am very pleased . . .

STEWART *slows down as he watches* ADA *again sign to* FLORA; *he has the uncomfortable impression he is being interrupted.*

FLORA: Mother wants to know if they could come back directly for it?

STEWART *is shocked; his mouth hangs slightly open, paused in mid-speech.* TAHU *mimics this mouth-drop perfectly.*

FLORA: . . . after they have taken the other things?

STEWART *is growing confused and anxious. His two mimics and their growing audience unnerve him further.*

23

PITO: *Kei Riri a te raho Maroke.* (*Shouted loudly at* TAHU.)

[*Subtitled*: Watch it, dry-balls is getting touchy.]

STEWART *nods suspiciously towards the* MAORI *speaker, not understanding him; the speaker smiles and nods back.*

STEWART: I suggest you prepare for a difficult journey. The bush will tear clothes and the mud is deep in places.

STEWART *walks away.* ADA *stands beside the piano, turned away from the activities.* FLORA *pats her hand trying to cheer her. Down on the beach a fire is lit and* pipis *are prepared for cooking. Some of the young men are racing naked into the sea.*

STEWART (*To* BAINES *about the* MAORIS.): What are they doing? We don't have time for that.

17. EXT. BEACH. DAY.

It is some hours later and the carrying party is beginning to make its way up into the bush. ADA *still stands beside her piano.* FLORA *wants to follow the party.* BAINES *comes back along the beach, trailed by a young Maori boy,* KAHA.

BAINES: Mr Stewart asked if I might show you to the path.

(ADA *does not move.*) . . . May I carry something?

ADA *turns to* BAINES, *her face angry and defiant, her eyes full of tears.* BAINES *falls back, struck by her show of emotion.* ADA *and* FLORA *walk past him towards the bush.*

18. EXT. BUSH AND CLIFF ABOVE BEACH. DAY.

The party threads its way through the bush along the cliff. ADA *pauses at the cliff top to see her piano below on the sand, tiny and desolate. Its distance and her love of it suddenly strike her. Its music is faint and becomes loud over the next scene.*

19. EXT. BUSH FROM BEACH. DAY.

Brown feet squelch through the mud, finally followed by dainty boots caked in dirt. The MAORI *leaders of the party have stopped.*

BAINES *works his way to the front.*[4]

BAINES: *E aha tenei?*

[*Subtitled*: What is it?]

HONE: *E hinga te Koroua ra a Pitama i konei. (Points.) Kare noa Kia hikina te tapu.*

[Old man Pitama died here. (*Points to the spot.*) The *Tapu* hasn't been lifted.]

STEWART *struggles up to the front to join* BAINES; *he speaks over the top of* HONE.

STEWART: What's he say?

BAINES: Someone died here. It's *tapu.*

STEWART: But we came down this way, didn't we? I'm sure we did.

The MAORI *leaders continue discussing:*

– Ol Pitama eh.

HONE: *E Tama heke atu ki raru – tiro hia atu. Rapuhia mai he huarahi re!*

[Go and look, find another track, eh!]

TIPI: *Kia tupato – he ana taniwha ke raro na.*

[*Subtitled*: Go easy, there's a ghost down there.]

HOTU: *Ka, rongo koe i te haunga o tana tutae i te tuatahi.*

[You'll smell his shit first.]

STEWART *continues over the top of the* MAORI *discussion.*

STEWART: They want more money. They are trying to make two days out of it?

BAINES: No, no, they know another track – to the side of this.

---

[4] See notes, p. 128.

ADA *and* FLORA *sit watching, out of breath. The bush is dense, claustrophobic and exotic. One of the* MAORI *women sits close to* ADA *apparently not looking at her. Slowly she draws the scarf that is in* ADA's *lap into her own. Defiantly she puts it on.*

Meanwhile another woman makes a very dignified attempt to wipe the freckles from FLORA's *face.*

20. EXT. STEWART'S HUT. DAY.
It is another day and STEWART's *hut, bleakly set amidst smoking stumps, is full of squeals, chasing and antics.*

21. INT. STEWART'S HUT. DAY.
The Reverend in frock coat has a wedding dress stuck part-way up his arms. It is not a normal wedding dress but a backless one used again and again as a photographic prop. Stewart's AUNT MORAG *and her companion* NESSIE *are trying to pull it off.*

AUNT MORAG: Watch your feet!

NESSIE: Watch your feet!

ADA *and* FLORA *find the family fun frightening and have taken refuge in the bedroom.*

AUNT MORAG: Careful! Watch his hand.

NESSIE: Watch his hand . . .

The REVEREND *tickles his sister as she tries to get the sleeve off his hand.* NESSIE *squeals with excitement.*

AUNT MORAG: *Stop* iiit!

NESSIE, *panting with excitement at the fun, looks towards* ADA.

AUNT MORAG (*Shooing the Reverend out.*): We'll bring out the bride.

The two women now fit the wedding dress on ADA.

AUNT MORAG: LIFT – YOUR – ARM – UP – DEAR.

FLORA *sits on the bed sulkily. She leans back and crosses her legs.*

FLORA: My REAL father was a famous German
    composer . . .

AUNT MORAG: . . . Ohh, the tag is broken.

FLORA (*Continues.*): . . . They met when my mother was
    an opera singer . . . in Luxemburg . . .

The two women pause to look at FLORA. ADA *signs to*
FLORA: *'THAT'S ENOUGH!'*

FLORA: Why?

ADA *looks away, the two women finish primping the dress.*
FLORA *crosses her arms.*

FLORA: I want to be in the photograph.

22. EXT. STEWART'S HUT. DAY.

NESSIE *half-holds an umbrella over* ADA *as they make their way to where the camera is set up in front of a chair and a sparse display of three toi-toi. All about the house is muddy, so that they must weave their way through on planks and logs. A fine veil of rain is falling across the distant bush, the whole valley is shrouded in mist.*

STEWART *looks through the camera at the* REVEREND *and the photographer who are posing as the couple, complete with tatty bouquet.* STEWART *notices* ADA's *arrival and, seeing her as a real bride, his bride, he is struck dumb with pride; even the rough tapes at the back of the dress cannot destroy the illusion.*

STEWART: . . . Beautiful.

The umbrellas are held away, the rain pours down.

23. INT./EXT. STEWART'S HUT/BEDROOM. DAY.

AUNT MORAG *has brought a chair into the bedroom and sits knee to knee with* FLORA.

AUNT MORAG: I thought she met your father in Luxemburg.

FLORA: Well, yes, in Austria, where he conducted the Royal Orchestra . . .

AUNT MORAG (*Frowning.*): And where did they get married?

AUNT MORAG *checks to see if someone is coming.*

FLORA (*Her Scottish accent becoming thick and expressive.*): In an enormous forest, with real fairies as bridesmaids each holding a little elf's hand.

AUNT MORAG *sits back, regarding* FLORA *with obvious disapproval and disappointment. She smooths back her hair.*

FLORA: No, I tell a lie, it was in a small country church, near the mountains . . .

AUNT MORAG *is becoming involved again. She leans forward.*

AUNT MORAG: Which mountains are those, dear?

FLORA: The Alps.

AUNT MORAG: Ohhh, I've never been there. (*She leans forward.*)

FLORA: Mother used to sing songs in German and her voice would echo across the valleys . . . That was before the accident . . .

AUNT MORAG: Oh, what happened?

AUNT MORAG *looks over her shoulder as* FLORA *continues to talk; so persuasive is* FLORA's *storytelling that the scene comes vividly to life, albeit in* FLORA's *dark pupil.*

FLORA: One day when my mother and father were singing together in the forest, a great storm blew up out of nowhere. But so passionate was their singing that they did not notice, nor did they stop as the rain began to fall, and when their voices rose for the final bars of the duet a great bolt of lightning came out of the sky and struck my father so that he lit up like a torch . . . And at the same moment my father was struck dead my mother was struck dumb! She – never – spoke – another – word.

AUNT MORAG: Ohhh . . . dear! Not another word . . . From the shock, yes it would be.

The story is interrupted by the return of the WEDDING PARTY, *who are dripping wet, exactly as the couple in the story.* AUNT MORAG *bustles over to take off the wet wedding gown, her face puckered with tragedy.*

AUNT MORAG: . . . Terrible . . . Terrible . . .

Before she can undo the ties ADA *pulls it from herself, so aggressively that the ties and part of the gown come apart. None of this is a concern to* ADA, *who is distracted with fear for her piano. She crosses to the little window and stares anxiously at the falling rain.*

24. EXT. BEACH. DUSK.
Soft piano music has been playing over the previous scene. Now it builds to strength as sea water swirls high around the piano, small and embattled on the dark, rainy beach.

25. INT. STEWART'S HUT/BEDROOM. DAY.
It's morning of the next day. ADA *and* FLORA *sit amongst tea chests in the bedroom.* ADA *is signing intently to* FLORA. FLORA *signs back, sometimes using words.* STEWART *watches, uneasy with their secret communication. As* STEWART *enters the animation is suspended.* ADA *stands and takes a step back, as if to attention.*

STEWART: I shall be gone for some days. There is some Maori land I want and may buy very reasonably.

(STEWART *shuffles*.) I am hoping you will use the time
  to settle in, and, in some ways, we may start again . . .
FLORA *and* ADA *look at each other.*
STEWART: All right?
ADA *looks at him blankly, then nods.*

26. EXT. STEWART'S HUT. DAY.
ADA *and* FLORA, *dressed in cloaks and bonnets, skirt the
dense bush trying to find a path in. It is not easy, because
the bush is so tight.* ADA's *leg slides in up to her calf in
mud.*

27. EXT. BAINES'S HUT. DAY.
ADA *and* FLORA *arrive at* BAINES's *hut. It is mid-morning
but* BAINES *is not yet dressed.* ADA *hands him a note.*
BAINES *looks at it blankly.*
BAINES: I'm not able to read.
ADA *signs to* FLORA.
FLORA: Please take us to the beach where we landed.
BAINES: I'm sorry, I can't do that. (FLORA *and* ADA *stare
  evenly at him.*) I don't have the time. (*They continue
  to stare.*) Goodbye . . .

28. EXT. BAINES'S HUT. DAY.
It is much later when BAINES *emerges from his hut with a
saddle over his arm. The two women are still there.* ADA
looks up at him expectantly. FLORA *mirrors her
expression.*
BAINES: I – can't – take – you – there. I can't do it.
*He puts the saddle over a rail. He continues to saddle up,
sneaking glances at them from under the horse and around
its side. They watch him closely, not pleadingly, but
stubbornly, eerily of one mind.*

29. EXT. BEACH. DAY.

The sky is blue with long wisps of cloud.

The party of three break on to the long expanse of beach where the piano still stands. It has not been without visitors. There are footprints on the sand and some of the boards have been pulled back. ADA *passes* BAINES, *walking urgently towards it. Soon,* ADA *has removed enough boards that she may lift the lid and play the keys.* BAINES *stays back.* ADA *takes great delight in feeling her fingers on the keys again. Her whole composition is altered. She is animated, joyful, excited.*

Down on the wet sand FLORA *does a wild dance of her own invention using a seaweed wig. She finishes by rolling down the beach in the sand.*

BAINES *views them with suspicion, yet he is magnetically drawn to the spectacle. He has never seen women behave with so much abandon. His attention fixes on* ADA's *uninhibited, emotional playing, and as he watches he finds himself edging irresistibly closer.*[5]

30. EXT. BEACH. LATE AFTERNOON.

The shadows are long on the sand when BAINES *collects the boards.* ADA *and* FLORA *are attempting a duet.*[6] ADA *notices him come towards them with the boards, obviously intending that they should leave. Her mood darkens, she continues playing stubbornly even though* FLORA *has stopped. Abruptly she finishes. In black spirits she replaces her cape and bonnet.* BAINES *is struck by this sudden change; he watches her mesmerized as he replaces the boards.*

[5-6] See notes, p. 129.

35

31. EXT. BUSH AND CLIFF ABOVE BEACH. DUSK.
Again ADA *stops to look at her piano from the cliff top. The sky is darkening and the air is full of bird calls. She turns from the cliff top, her face grimly set. She walks past* BAINES, *oblivious of his curiosity.*

32. EXT. STEWART'S HUT. DUSK.
STEWART *walks along the lip of the hill in evening silhouette. Down below, the hut puffs smoke out into the valley. The lie of the land traps sound like a shell, and the clear, high notes of a voice echo out.*

33. EXT./INT. STEWART'S HUT AND KITCHEN. DUSK.
Suspicious that ADA *is singing,* STEWART *approaches the house quietly. Through the open kitchen door he sees that the keys of a piano have been etched on the table top. While* ADA *'plays' the notes* FLORA *sings them.*[7]

STEWART *puts his pack down.* ADA *stands to attention, folding the tablecloth back over the table.*
STEWART: Hello, then.
FLORA: Hello.
ADA *nods.* STEWART's *hand explores the markings on the table.* ADA *watches his hand moving under the checked cloth.*

34. INT. MISSION HOUSE. DAY.
AUNT MORAG, NESSIE *and* TWO MAORI GIRLS *dressed in proper Victorian costume are kneeling around a huge double white sheet, sewing and cutting it. The* MAORI GIRLS *are part of the mission's good works. They are dressed in European style and while their training is in*

[7] See notes, p. 129.

*polite, proper, domestic behaviour they constantly corrupt
it with their demonstrative displays of affection, and their
clay tobacco pipes to which they are addicted.*

STEWART *is standing, looking on.* BAINES *is behind him
in the kitchen removing his boots.*

AUNT MORAG (*Looking carefully at* STEWART.): Well, you
stopped combing your hair, which is a good thing, it
was looking over-done. (*Without pause, but referring to
the sheet.*) You see, these are the slits that the heads will
go through, show him, Nessie . . . they'll be dead, the
Reverend is going to use animal blood, no doubt it will
be very dramatic. Tea! (*For* NESSIE *rather than to her.*)

NESSIE: It will be very dramatic.

NESSIE *leaves to get the tea.* HENI, *the* MAORI GIRL *with a
moku, tickles* MARY's *back while she sews.*

They sing the anthem in snatches.[8] *It is background to
the conversation.*

STEWART (*Sitting down.*): What would you think if
someone played a kitchen table like it were a piano?

AUNT MORAG: Like it were a piano?

STEWART: It's strange, isn't it? I mean, it's not a piano, it
doesn't make any sound.

NESSIE *puts* STEWART's *tea down.* BAINES *comes in with
his tea cup, which is dwarfed by his big hands. He stands
back, leaning against a wall.*

AUNT MORAG (*Hissing to* NESSIE): Biscuits! No, no sound.

NESSIE *hustles back to the kitchen.*

STEWART: I knew she was mute, but now I'm thinking it's
more than that. I'm wondering if she's not brain-
affected.

AUNT MORAG: . . . No sound at all?

[8] See notes, p. 129.

39

STEWART: No, it was a table.

AUNT MORAG (*Musing.*): Well, she was very violent with the gown. She tore off a chunk of lace. If I hadn't been there I'd have sworn she'd used her teeth . . .

NESSIE: . . . and wiped her feet on it.

STEWART: Well, it has not yet come to anything, just a concern.

AUNT MORAG pats her chest, a calming device.

AUNT MORAG: Oh, yes, yes of course, a concern.

STEWART: There is something to be said for silence . . .

AUNT MORAG: Oh indeed. Cotton!

She holds up her needle for NESSIE *to thread.*

STEWART (*Warming.*): . . . And with time she will, I'm sure, become affectionate.

AUNT MORAG: Certainly, there is nothing so easy to like as a pet, and *they are quite silent.*

BAINES *watches quietly on.*

35. EXT. STEWART'S WOODCHOP. DAY.

STEWART *is at the woodchop cutting firewood. He displays his virtuosity as an axeman, cutting the wood into ever more slender pieces.* FLORA *is watching and stacking the fallen timber. She flinches as the axe hits the wood, but scurries in to pick up the timber.* BAINES *is standing talking to* STEWART.

BAINES: Those eighty acres, that cross the stream, what do you think of them?

STEWART: On your property?

BAINES: Yes.

BAINES *carries a log across for* STEWART, *who talks without pausing in his work.*

STEWART: Good, flattish land with reliable water – why? I don't have money. What are you about?

40

BAINES: I'd like to make a swap.

STEWART: What for?

BAINES: The piano.

STEWART: The piano on the beach? Ada's piano?

BAINES *nods.* STEWART *stops; this is serious.*

STEWART: It's not marshy is it?

STEWART *has walked a few paces away from his woodchop in the direction of the land.*

BAINES: No.

STEWART: You'd have to organize it up here.

BAINES: Yes, I thought that.

STEWART: Well, Baines the music lover, I never would have known. Hidden talents, George.

BAINES: I'll have to get lessons. It wouldn't be much use without them.

STEWART: Yes, I suppose you would.

BAINES *remains silent. He looks away.*

STEWART: Well, Ada can play.

BAINES *shrugs.*

STEWART: I have it in a letter she plays well. She's been playing since she was 5 or 6.

FLORA *has stopped stacking. She is lying along the top of the wood, lifting a leg up and down, watching the men.*

36. INT. STEWART'S KITCHEN. DAY.

STEWART, *flushed with his plans, is pouring tea into cups.* FLORA *peers at cup level through the steam.* ADA *sits beside her at the table.*

STEWART: I have got us some excellent land. Baines has taken some queer idea to have a piano, and you are to give him lessons. Have you taught before?

ADA *signs to* FLORA.

FLORA: What on?

41

STEWART: On your piano, that is the swap.

ADA *finger-signs, her face furious.*

STEWART: What does she say?

FLORA: She says it's her piano, and she won't have him touch it. He's an oaf, he can't read, he's ignorant.

STEWART: He wants to improve himself . . . and you will be able to play it . . . (ADA *is not responding well.*) Teach him to look after it.

ADA*'s breathing becomes heavy with anger, she writes furiously on her pad: 'NO, NO, THE PIANO IS MINE! IT'S MINE!'*

STEWART *regards her note and her passion with suspicion and disdain.*

STEWART (*Getting up.*): You can't go on like this, we are a family now, all of us make sacrifices and so will you.

ADA*'s anger explodes, she sweeps the cups, teapot, bread, off the table.* STEWART *walks out white-faced and stiff.* FLORA *stoops to pick up the cups, but quickly steps back as* ADA *impulsively hurls a plate after the retreating* STEWART. *The plate smashes on the wall.* STEWART *returns, shaking with anger.*

STEWART: You will teach him. I shall see to that!

ADA*'s emotions are suddenly removed and she views* STEWART *blankly, eerily.*

37. EXT. BUSH FROM BEACH. DAY.

The piano is taken up through the bush by a group of six to eight MAORI MEN. *It's very heavy and awkward and they grunt and struggle with it.*

   Hiki na ake muri na!
   [Lift up the back.]
   Tero – tero!
   [Arsehole!]

Hei niti niti maau! (Turning around.)
[You lick it.]
Someone stumbles and the back of the piano comes crashing to the ground, thundering out in the bottom end of the scale. People scatter. Only TU *stays, who warrior-like challenges the piano in a* haka:

> *Kowai tenei e haruru nei?*
> *Ko Ruaumoko, Ko Ruaumoko.*
> *Kowai tenei e haruru nei!*
> *Ko Ruaumoko, Ko Ruaumoko.*
> *Werohia Patúa, Werohia Patúa*
> *Werohia Patúa – Werohia Patúa*
> *Te Taniwha, Te Taniwha.*
> *Kei roto ra ee He!*[9]

One of the other MAORIS *comes forward cautiously. He lifts a corner of the piano and drops it. The piano rings out, the sound carrying across a great sweep of bush.*

38. EXT. PATH TO BAINES'S HUT THROUGH BEARDED FOREST. DAY.
The women duck low to avoid a branch as STEWART *leads them to* BAINES's *hut on his horse. The path slopes up through a strange, bearded forest where the tops of trees are bare and ghost-like.*
STEWART: I'd try children's tunes, nothing more complicated . . .
ADA *is unrepentant, she does not want to teach* BAINES *the piano.*
STEWART: Just be encouraging, no one expects him to be good.

[9] See notes, p. 129.

39. INT./EXT. BAINES'S HUT. DAY.

The piano is the only cared-for item in the rough hut.

STEWART (*Lifting the lid.*): It looks good, very nice-
looking thing. Well . . . I wish you luck. The girls are
very excited about the lessons.

The 'girls' look anything but excited. FLORA, *shy, plays
obsessively with a long strand of greasy hair.* ADA *is cold
and grim.*

STEWART: Flora will explain anything Ada says. They talk
through their fingers, you can't believe what they say
with just their hands.

STEWART *leaves.* BAINES *goes to the piano and lifts the
lid. He looks at them.* ADA *signs to* FLORA.

FLORA: My mother wants to see your hands. Hold them
out.

BAINES *holds out his hands, spread wide as if holding a
ball.*

FLORA: No, no, like this . . .

FLORA *puts her neat little fingers together, first with their
backs up, then she turns them over.* BAINES *does the same,
only his hands are big and coarse.* ADA *signs to* FLORA.
BAINES *is shyly keen.*

FLORA: You have to wash them.

BAINES: They are washed.

ADA *signs.*

FLORA: Wash them again.

BAINES: The marks do not come off. They are scars and
hardened skin.

ADA *and* FLORA *do not move. Humiliated,* BAINES *takes a
scrub brush, soap and bucket and goes outside, followed
by* FLORA. ADA *can see him from the window. She moves
to her piano. She wants to touch it but she is torn by her
feelings, wanting it, but not owning it. She strokes the*

varnished wood with her hand and softly lifts the lid. *Outside,* FLORA *stands beside* BAINES, *pointing out bits of his hands he should still scrub. Furtively* ADA *lays her hands on the keys. The instrument is horribly out of tune, almost every note is off. She goes outside and signs to* FLORA.

FLORA: There's no tune left in the piano so she can't teach you.

The two women leave.

40. EXT. STEEP BUSH HILL. DAY.

Two men come crashing out down a steep bush hill. They are tied to each other. BAINES, *the younger and stronger, is trying to break their fall by grasping hold of branches and shoots. Finally their fall is checked. The old man is white-haired, the front of his suit splattered with the debris of many meals. He sits up, feeling about for his glasses. He is blind. His eyes, though closed, wobble and roll.* BAINES *finds the glasses. One of the lenses has gone, the other is very dark. The old man fits his handkerchief in the gap.*

41. EXT. HUGE SCREE. DAY.

BAINES *carries the old man on his back; they cross a huge scree. Each of* BAINES'S *steps dislodges a fall of rocks. The crashing of stones echoes across the valley.* BAINES *and he are but small dots in this giant earth scar.*

42. EXT. CABBAGE-TREE MARSH. DAY.

BAINES *has a long stick in each hand. The white-haired man holds on to each from behind. His feet search for safe footing. The place they walk in is full of cabbage trees and marshy ground.*

47

43. INT. BAINES'S HUT. DAY.

Inside BAINES's *hut, the old man feels the piano.*

BLIND MAN: Ah, a . . . Broadbent. A fine instrument. I've not come across one here, or in the Islands where I have tuned some two hundred. Yes, they like their pianos there.

Out of his pocket he takes a carefully wrapped tuning fork. He unwraps the package, lifts the back and lid and starts to tune. He sniffs the air. BAINES *watches. He sniffs close to the keys:*

Scent? And salt of course.

He works on.

What will you play when it's tuned? What music do you play?

BAINES *looks over at him from the meal he is preparing.*

BAINES: I can't play.

The blind man stops working.

BLIND MAN: You don't play?

BAINES: No, I can't. I'm going to learn.

The man goes back to work somewhat depressed by the futility of the venture.

BLIND MAN: Well my dear Miss Broadbent, tuned, but silent.

44. EXT. BAINES'S HUT AND CHIMNEY. NIGHT.

The hut's chimney spits sparks and flames into the night air.

45. INT. BAINES'S HUT. NIGHT.

Inside, the two men eat a plain meal of pork and potatoes. The blind man eats off a box top. BAINES *has his meal on his lap. His dog watches each fork-load to his mouth. A big cloud of smoke hangs in the room.*

BLIND MAN: My wife sang with a bell-clear tone. After we
married she stopped. She said she didn't feel like
singing, that life made her sad. And that's how she
lived, lips clamped closed over a perfect voice, a
beautiful voice.

46. INT. BAINES'S HUT. MORNING.
*A slash of sunlight falls across the piano. Thousands of
particles of dust become visible floating in the air. BAINES
is at the window in his shirt/nightshirt. He notices the dust
on the piano and strips off his shirt, which he uses as a
duster. Under the shirt he is naked. As he wipes the
smooth wood he becomes aware of his nakedness. His
movements become slower until he is no longer cleaning,
but caressing the piano.*

47. EXT. PATH TO BAINES'S HUT. DAY.
On the path to BAINES's *house,* ADA *and* FLORA *sit in the
bush.* ADA's *head is bowed. Her hands held over her face.*
FLORA *tries to catch the spots of light in her palm as they
twinkle through the thick canopy of leaves overhead.*

48. EXT./INT. BAINES'S HUT. DAY.
The door opens. ADA *and* FLORA *stand in their cloaks and
bonnets.*
FLORA: Mother says she can't stand to teach piano with it
all out of tune. So I'm to do scales.
ADA *turns and walks off.* FLORA *bustles in.* BAINES
watches ADA *from the window.*
FLORA: I hope you've scrubbed your hands.
FLORA *begins a scale.*
        Oh, it's in tune.
She looks over at BAINES, *who is still gazing out of the
window.*

49

FLORA: What's out there?

She gets up to see what BAINES *is looking at. She sees her mother and divines* BAINES *is looking at nothing.*

FLORA: You have to watch me where I put my fingers.

FLORA *starts again.* ADA *can only hear the piano faintly but moves closer as she too hears it is in tune.*

As she enters the hut BAINES *pulls his fingers away from the piano.* FLORA *sees this and stops too. She looks at her mother.*

FLORA: It's in tune.

ADA *checks the other notes.* FLORA *stands with her arms folded, a bit sulky and fluffed up.*

FLORA (*Hissing.*): I was teaching.

ADA *tries the piano. She looks over at* BAINES, *then signs to* FLORA.

FLORA: She wants to see what you can do.

BAINES: I'd rather not play. I want to listen and learn that way.

FLORA: Everyone has to practise.

BAINES: I just want to listen.

ADA *is a bit nonplussed. She does not want to be listened to any more than she wants to teach. She pulls a strand of her hair, then signs to* FLORA.

FLORA: What do you want to hear?

BAINES *shrugs shyly and looks away out of the window. He doesn't know.*

BAINES: Anything.

ADA *is slow to start. Unobliging as ever she plays scales. But once begun her belligerence fades as her absorption in the music strengthens.*

49. INT. STEWART'S HUT/ADA'S BEDROOM. NIGHT.
Back at STEWART'S *hut,* ADA *lies dispirited on the bed.*

FLORA *lies beside her holding* ADA's *hand.*

FLORA: Tell me about my real father, tell me that story.

ADA *signs.*

> Ohh, but tell me again. Was he your teacher?

ADA *nods and strokes* FLORA's *hair from her face.* FLORA *lies back.*

> How did you speak to him.

ADA *signs to* FLORA, *who watches, in love with all the stories of her real and unreal father.*

ADA: [*Subtitled*: I didn't need to speak, I could lay thoughts out in his mind like they were a sheet.]

FLORA: What happened? Why didn't you get married?

ADA *continues to sign, her hands casting odd, animal-like shadows on the newspapered walls.*

ADA (*cont.*): [*Subtitled*: After a while he became frightened and he stopped listening.]

FLORA (*Signing.*): Then I was born?

ADA *nods.*

FLORA (*Speaking.*): And he was sent away. I think . . .

ADA *has her hand on* FLORA's *mouth;* FLORA *takes it away, curls up around it like a pillow.*

> I think he's looking for us now all across the world, across the red sea.

STEWART *enters their bedroom.* FLORA *stops and* ADA *stands against the wall.* STEWART *finds the atmosphere curious yet impenetrable.*

STEWART: Shall I kiss you goodnight?

FLORA *looks up at her mother.* ADA *shrugs.*

> STEWART *nods stiffly; uncomfortably, he leaves.*

50. EXT. BAINES'S VERANDAH. DAY.

It is raining heavily. FLORA *sits on the small verandah outside* BAINES's *hut, her legs stuck straight out into the wet. She is operating a merciless power game with the dog, forcing it out of the verandah with a stick.*

51. INT. BAINES'S HUT. DAY.

ADA*'s playing can be heard.* BAINES *sits back watching* ADA. *Her cape on the hook is dripping a puddle on to the floor and there is a circle of drips around her skirt hem. She is totally absorbed in her piano music as she was on the beach.*

BAINES *watches. Her long white neck, now wet from rain, proves irresistible. He comes across the room and kisses her.* ADA *jumps up and prepares to leave.* BAINES *stands in front of the door.*

BAINES: Do you know how to bargain? Nod if you do.
She doesn't move.

> There's a way you can have your piano back. Do you
> want it back? . . . You want it back?

ADA *eyes him suspiciously.*

BAINES: You see, I'd like to us to make a deal. There's
> things I want to do while you play. If you let me you
> can earn it back.

> What do you think, one visit for every key?

ADA *is tense but she is thinking about it. She holds up a finger then points to the black of her dress.*

BAINES: Your dress?

ADA *shakes her head.*

> Skirt . . . ?

She walks over to her piano and points to a black key.

> For every black one?

ADA *turns, raising her head, nodding.*

> That's a lot less, half.

BAINES *is counting the keys.* ADA *starts for the front door.*

> All right, all right then, the black keys.

She sits back at the piano. She plays the lowest black key as in 'number one'.

She takes her hands off the piano, waiting.

It's better that you play.

Obediently she begins, stopping abruptly, indignantly, as he touches her neck.

BAINES: Play . . . Keep playing.

After a moment she settles back to the piano.

52. EXT. BAINES'S VERANDAH. DAY.

Outside FLORA *is cradling the poor confused dog, asking him what cruel miserable person sent him out into the cold and wet.*

53. EXT. RIVERHOLE NEAR BAINES'S HUT. DAY.

BAINES *bathes in a riverhole. He is watched by a gathering of Maoris, sometimes with great seriousness, at other times with hilarity. They pass between them his clothes, trying them on and mimicking him. One of the older women,* HIRA, *crouches close to the bank keeping up a steady line of enquiry. Her manner is relaxed but focused and persistent. She smokes a pipe.*

HIRA: I got the good wife for you, *Peini*. She pray good.
   Clean. Read Bible. You sleep her, *Peini*. She chief
   daughter.

BAINES: No, no Bible readers.

BAINES *continues good-humouredly washing.*

HIRA: Why? We need you *pakeha* clever. You sleep her.

TAHU (*A big man dressed as a woman.*): (*Background.*) I
   give her plenty clever. (*Gestures sexually.*)

BAINES: I have a wife.

TAHU (*Camping it up.*): I give her clever, eh *Peini*.
   Hallelujah!

HIRA: Don't answer, he low-born. Jus' look at him, mongrel. Your wife where she?

BAINES: She lives her own life in New Jersey, America.

HIRA: You have spare wife here, *Peini*. You get *mana* for that. Our chief he four wives.

BAINES *shakes his head, amused. As he gets out of the river* HIRA *slaps him.*

I marry white man, *Peini*, he a whaler like you. He very good to me. Love me, nurse me.

HIRA *touches her own face where* BAINES'*s tattoo is.*

HIRA: Who do that? It not finish, that no good, *Peini*. You finish!

Several people on the bank are taking turns to comb their hair, peering into a tiny piece of mirror.

54. EXT./INT. BAINES'S HUT. DAY.

BAINES'*s dog hears* ADA *and* FLORA *approach. It takes off under the house.* FLORA *calls the dog. It keeps well hidden.* ADA *has gone on inside and the door is closed.* FLORA *stands outside the door, left out and lonely. She knocks.* BAINES *answers.*

FLORA (*Small voice.*): I want to speak to my mother.

She buries her head in her mother's skirt.

I don't want to be outside, I want to watch.

ADA *signs to* FLORA.

I'll be very quiet.

ADA *leads her to the door, signing to her.*

I won't look at him!

FLORA *is shut out.*

55. INT. BAINES'S HUT. DAY.

ADA *sits at the piano. She is shy and nervous. She turns to* BAINES, *who nods.* ADA *begins to play.* BAINES *keeps his head bowed, but as the playing becomes more confident he raises his head to watch. He sits at a far corner of the room, apparently enjoying the whole vision of this woman at her piano.*

After some time BAINES, *affected by the music, takes his chair to a closer position and from an opposite angle.* ADA *glances up as she feels him passing behind her. He seems satisfied to watch. His attention finally focuses on her neck as it bends further from or closer to the piano.*

Again he shifts his chair, taking it round the back and to the other side of the piano. As he moves ADA *watches warily. From this position he doesn't try to touch her, but watches, enjoying her fingers moving on the keys and the small details of emotion on her face. Twice he closes his eyes and breathes deeply.* BAINES *is experiencing an unpractised sense of appreciation and lust. When his eyes are closed,* ADA *glances at him with curiosity and suspicion.*

56. INT. SCHOOL HALL. DAY.
FLORA *stands on a kitchen chair.* AUNT MORAG *and* NESSIE *have paused from fitting* FLORA's *bodice and wire angel wings. They are attempting to learn the hand gestures as* FLORA *signs:*

'I shall listen hard to rehearsal, because I live too far away to go often.'

AUNT MORAG (*Suspiciously*): Which sign is the word rehearsal?

FLORA *deftly demonstrates.*

AUNT MORAG: I can't imagine a fate worse than being dumb. Turn around.

NESSIE: To be deaf?

AUNT MORAG: Oh yes, deaf too – *terrible! Awful!*

FLORA: Actually, to tell you the whole truth, Mama says

most people speak rubbish and it's not worth the
listen.
AUNT MORAG *and* NESSIE *exchange looks.*
AUNT MORAG (*Stiffly.*): Well, that is a strong opinion.
FLORA: Yes, it's unholy.

57. INT. BAINES'S HUT. DAY.
ADA *is quick to remove a used plate and cup left on top of
the piano.* BAINES *is sitting next to the window, his elbow
on the sill, his head turned away.*
BAINES: Lift your skirt.
ADA *stops playing. She turns to him. Thinks about it, then
slowly lifts her skirt a little to show her boots.*
    Lift it higher.
ADA *pulls the skirts up fractionally so the tops of her
boots are exposed.* BAINES *nods.* ADA *starts to play again,
not so confidently as before.* BAINES *moves close, he goes
down on his knees to watch her feet on the pedals.*
BAINES: Higher.
ADA *doesn't hear.*
    Lift it higher.
She stops and lifts her skirt to her knees. She looks at
BAINES *with ill-disguised contempt.* BAINES *is enthralled
with her legs, or what he can now see of them. He moves
back to watch them from behind. He's lying on the
ground, head propped on his arm.* ADA's *slim stockinged
calves work the pedals; one of the stockings has a small
hole through which her white skin shows.*

58. EXT. MISSION HOUSE. DUSK.
Outside the Mission House HENI *holds* STEWART's *horse.
Its wet coat steams in the night air, making the whole
horse glow.* HENI *talks softly to it in Maori.*

59. INT. MISSION HOUSE. NIGHT.

Inside the REVEREND *is closely watched by* STEWART,
AUNT MORAG *and* NESSIE *as he cuts out the shape of an
axe from a piece of marbled cardboard. A lamplight
flickers warm tones across their faces while the rest of the
room is dark, giving it a conspiratorial air.*

REVEREND: Nessie, your hand out . . . out here, please.

NESSIE: Oh, no, use Stewart, I can't act.

REVEREND: Nessie, please.

NESSIE *hesitatingly puts her arm out towards him and the*
REVEREND *chops away in the air two feet in front of her.*
NESSIE *looks at* AUNT MORAG, *puzzled.*

REVEREND: Look, you are being attacked!

The REVEREND *points to the opposite rose-papered wall,
where his shadow and paper axe now look very real as
they loom large above the crouching* NESSIE, *chopping into
her.* NESSIE *squeals, as does* MARY.

REVEREND: And with the blood . . . it will be a good
    effect.

60. INT. BAINES'S HUT. DAY.

ADA's *finger plays the fourth black key from the left-hand
side, denoting lesson four.*

BAINES: Undo your dress. This part – (*He indicates the
    top.*) I want to see your arms.

ADA *is taken unawares. She sits a moment, unsure if she
wants to co-operate, then slowly she starts to undo her
buttons.*

ADA *pulls her arms out of the tight sleeves. Underneath
she wears a worn-in bodice. Her arms are so white they
seem transparent. A delicate network of blue-green veins
crisscross up the soft underpart of her arms. A dark
growth of hair in her armpit suggests a shadowy depth.*

*The backs of her hands, normally white, are quite tanned
in comparison.*
BAINES: Play.

BAINES *draws his chair close. Gently he places his hand on
the soft underpart of her forearm.* ADA *stiffens and pulls
away. He grips the arm.*

Two keys.

ADA *continues to play. Slowly he moves his hand higher
towards her shoulder. Clearly unnerved, she changes the
music to something brisk, almost comical.* BAINES *feels
suddenly ridiculous, his mood broken. He takes his hand
away and moves back to the window, injured.* ADA *is
victorious, she is pleased to have won herself a respite.*

61. EXT. STEWART'S WOODCHOP. DAY.

STEWART *is at the woodchop talking to* AUNT MORAG
and NESSIE. MARY *and* HENI, AUNT MORAG'*s Maori girls,
lie sprawled out under a tree.*

AUNT MORAG: I hardly need to give one to you, but there
    you are anyway.

NESSIE *has been sorting through a basket of invitations;
finding* STEWART'*s, she hands it to* AUNT MORAG, *who
hands it to* STEWART.

    Don't be late. You will see there are two times, and
    since you are accompanying a performer you will need
    to make the earlier time . . .

STEWART *has stopped listening; he is watching* ADA *and*
FLORA *pick their way through the fallen logs to* BAINES'*s
path.*

STEWART: Wait.

*The two women stop. There is a Japanese sense of
deferment to* STEWART.

STEWART: How are the lessons going?

ADA *nods enthusiastically.*

He's getting on all right?

ADA *nods again.*

Good.

AUNT MORAG: That is good, yes.

As ADA *walks on,* AUNT MORAG *leans towards* STEWART.

She seems quietened down. Is she more affectionate?

STEWART *looks after them, unable to answer.*

AUNT MORAG: Ah well, slowly, slowly . . . Mary, Heni . . .

But they don't move.

NESSIE: Shall I tickle them?

AUNT MORAG: Yes, try that.

62. INT. BAINES'S HUT. DAY.

BAINES *secures a chair against the door while* ADA *is removing her dress top. She sits at the piano, hugging herself against the chill. As* BAINES *passes he knocks the jacket off the chair back. He picks it up and takes it across to her seat by the window.*

BAINES *nods and* ADA *begins to play.* BAINES *fingers the still warm jacket, he lifts it up and smells it.* ADA *turns around and stops playing, suddenly appalled by his odd sensual pleasure-taking. She holds out her hand for the jacket, her expression stern and censorious. She indicates he should return it to the chair back.* BAINES *ignores her.* ADA *stands and comes over to* BAINES. *She pulls the jacket from his hands and replaces it across the chair back, but as she turns to sit* BAINES *is beside her. He pulls the shoulders of her bodice down, exposing her shoulders and some of her breast.* ADA *immediately stands, but* BAINES *is much stronger and man-handles her across to the bed.* ADA *struggles seriously; this is much, much more than she was expecting.*

BAINES: Ada, four keys.

ADA *holds up five fingers and mouths 'five'.*

I just want to lie.

ADA *shakes her head vigorously and again mouths 'five'.*

All right, all right, five.

ADA *no longer struggles. She is stiff and still.* BAINES, *intoxicated by the smell and presence of her skin, becomes soft and gentle. He kisses and touches her with feeling and affection. Then, suddenly aware of her stillness, he too becomes still. He pulls himself up to see whether her face betrays her feelings.* ADA *seizes this opportunity to return to the uncertain sanctuary of her piano. From the bed,* BAINES *watches her run a hand noiselessly over the polished ivory keys, a gesture betraying affection never afforded to him.* BAINES *gets up. He shuts the piano lid, forcing* ADA *to remove her hand.*

ADA *immediately stands and dresses, marking hurtfully* BAINES'S *ownership of her piano.*

63. EXT. STEWART'S HUT. SUNSET.

A golden evening. STEWART *in his best shirt and trousers prepares the horse and cart.*

64. INT. STEWART'S HUT/ADA'S BEDROOM. SUNSET.

Inside, FLORA *is in her finished angel costume; she sings softly to herself while* ADA *undoes the long strands of plaits and separates them to comb.*

FLORA: The Holly and the Ivy . . .

STEWART *comes in to put on his jacket, but the collar is all tucked in.* ADA *automatically adjusts it for him, settling it around his neck. Her touch, meant practically, strangely affects him. In an impassioned impulse, meant gallantly, he tries to kiss* ADA's *fingertips. The gesture falters as* ADA, *surprised, jumps back.*

65. EXT. SCHOOL HALL. DUSK.
People are arriving at the school hall.[10] *One family is being ferried through the mud in a wheelbarrow.*

66. INT. SCHOOL HALL. NIGHT.
Some people are already seated in the hall. Several other angels have arrived, and they, like FLORA, *are ushered backstage.*

67. INT. SCHOOL HALL/BACKSTAGE. NIGHT.
Backstage, the Sunday School teacher is gathering the children together, reminding them of the order of songs, checking their hair, etc. The local dramatic society are also preparing themselves. One of the women is peeping through a hole in a makeshift curtain to watch the townspeople seating themselves.
WOMAN: They're bringing in extra seats!
Despite this, there would still be only a maximum of forty people, ten or so of them MAORIS *in their best European dress.*
ANOTHER WOMAN: Oh God, don't pin my hair too high, Alfred!
STILL ANOTHER: Yes, me too, do it about here . . . (*She shows Alfred.*)
Two of the women are putting a little colouring on each of the angels while two other angels are being smacked for putting their white-gloved hands in the bucket of blood.

68. INT. SCHOOL HALL. NIGHT.
Everyone is chatting at each other's seats, except the MAORI *guests, who wait solemnly.* AUNT MORAG *is*

[10] See notes, p. 129.

organizing the placement of the new seats. BAINES *arrives.*

MAN ONE: Look who's here, the musical Mr Baines . . .
    What will we have tonight, George . . . 'Twinkle,
    twinkle'?

BAINES *smiles and blinks; the teasing continues as* BAINES
scans the room for ADA. *Two of the* MAORI PARTY *share
one pair of shoes so that only one may be in the hall at a
time, while the other waits barefoot outside.*

ANOTHER MAN: 'Mary had a little lamb' or a polka, come
    on, George, what's it to be?

AUNT MORAG *bustles over to* BAINES *and pushes him in
front of her towards* NESSIE *and the piano.*

AUNT MORAG: Mr Baines, do come and turn pages . . .

BAINES *looks wildly about for rescue.*

BAINES: . . . I can't read music, I have just begun.

BAINES *backs off from* NESSIE, *whose face drops in
disappointment. He has spotted* ADA *and is eager to take a
seat near her. He takes the seat next but one to* ADA. *He
sits, smiling and blinking. The teasing continues behind
him.*

STEWART (*Turning.*): Lot of fools. Come on, move up.

ADA *puts her hand on the seat and shakes her head,
indicating that she is saving it for* FLORA. BAINES *is
rebuffed and looks across at* ADA, *who ignores him.*

    *The main lights are put out and everyone returns to
their places. In the dark* STEWART *shyly takes* ADA's *hand
in his.* BAINES *watches* STEWART *squeezing her hand and,
quite out of control, stands and leaves, accompanied by a
chorus of 'Shhhhhhhhhhhhh'. Satisfied,* ADA *watches him
go.*

    *The children file on with their candles. They stand in a
group singing with great seriousness, but struck with
shyness their voices are so small as barely to be heard.*

64

– Sing up, Billy!

– Come on, sing out!

*One of the smallest promptly pees. An arm reaches under
the curtain to wipe the stage.*

69. INT. SCHOOL HALL AND BACKSTAGE. NIGHT.

*Backstage all is ready for the main dramatic event. There
seem to be more peep-holes than curtains as eyes press
themselves to the little flap. The master of ceremonies, the*
REVEREND, *is on stage explaining the dramatics. He is
wearing harlequin tights and rompers, his face is
dramatically paled. The candles are blown out.*

REVEREND: And so the young maid came upon each and
    all of Bluebeard's missing wives, their severed heads
    still bleeding, their eyes still crying.

*The piano accompaniment is suspenseful while the audience
shriek appreciatively. Backstage* AUNT MORAG *provides the
dripping blood; moving between the corpses, she peers at
the audience through a peep-hole in the curtain.*

REVEREND: But who is this? (AUNT MORAG *looks around
    gasping, fooled despite herself.*)

A loud improvised door-slam and heavy footsteps. NESSIE,
*in costume, freezes. The shadow of Bluebeard moves
clumsily down the cut-out banister and along the corridor.*

BLUEBEARD: I am home early, my sweet wife . . . where
    art thou?

*The girl scrambles for the fallen key and rushes out of the
closet into the silhouette corridor.*

YOUNG WIFE: Hello, husband, what a surprise!

BLUEBEARD: Yes, wife, a surprise indeed! So now you
    know my secret, you, the sweetest and youngest of all
    my wives, must prepare to take her place.

BLUEBEARD *pulls out a cut-out axe and moves towards*

her. Two of the young warriors in CHIEF NIHE's *party rise to their feet.*

> *Aue! Ha aha ra tenei?*
>
> [*Subtitled*: Hey! What's this?]
>
> *E Nihe, E Nihe he Kohuru, he kohuru?*
>
> [*Subtitled*: Nihe, Nihe, is this murder?]

NIHE *waves them down, but they are shaken up and only crouch above their seats. The others stare anxiously between* NIHE *and the stage.*

NIHE (*Amused by them.*): *E te whanau keite pai-he takaro tenei.*

> [*Subtitled*: Everything is fine, this is just a game.]

BLUEBEARD *moves closer; the young wife drops to her knees, her hands held up in prayer.*

YOUNG WIFE: No, no, wait!

BLUEBEARD: I shall not wait. Bare your neck.

As BLUEBEARD *raises his axe again, first one then the other of the young warriors run forward, shouting a fierce war cry and parting the audience, who flee to either side while the corpses come very much to life.*

> *Kia hiwara! Kia hiwara!*
>
> [*Subtitled*: Be on the alert! Brace yourself!]
>
> *Pokokohua – whakaputa mai ia koe!*
>
> [*Subtitled*: Coward! Show yourself, come out!]

Only NIHE *and his top-hatted daughter remain calmly in their seats. The warriors have* BLUEBEARD *cornered and whimpering, an umbrella held spear-like above him.* NIHE *stomps his stick, his great voice booming out.*

NIHE: *Hoki mai! Hoki mai!*

> [*Subtitled*: Come back here! Come back here!]

70. INT. SCHOOL HALL/BACKSTAGE. NIGHT.

Backstage the CHIEF *and his party are shown the theatrical devices; the blood-bucket, the paper axe, the splits in the sheets.*

71. INT. BAINES'S HUT. DAY.
ADA *goes to the piano; she is upset that* BAINES *has again left a plate on top of it.* BAINES *intercepts her, stepping several times between her and the piano. She sees the game and stands still. He steps aside. She removes the plate, lovingly wiping the surface underneath. There is a sulky irritation in the way* BAINES *watches her.*
BAINES: I have been waiting. You are very late.
ADA *starts to play;* BAINES *watches, then looks away.*
BAINES: I don't want you to play. I just want you to sit.
ADA *keeps playing until she has finished. Without looking at him she holds up two fingers against the piano.*
BAINES (*Angry.*): No, not two keys.
ADA *starts playing again;* BAINES *feels powerless. He no longer admires her absorption with the piano, he is jealous of it.*
BAINES (*Shouts.*): Two keys then!
She stops playing. There is an insolence or casualness in the way she regards BAINES. *He pulls her chair back from the piano. This upsets her, as much of her confidence was associated with the instrument.* BAINES *kisses her passionately on the mouth.* ADA *pulls back,* BAINES *persists, he is desperate and romantic.*

72. EXT. BASE OF BUSH-COVERED HILL. DAY.
STEWART, *with* BAINES *interpreting, talks with a group of* MAORIS *at the base of a bush-covered hill. The* MAORIS *sit behind a small representation of the hill marked out with twigs on the ground. The atmosphere is tense.*
MAORI NEGOTIATOR (*Pointing to the places.*): Nga awa
    kau kau, nga ana koiwi o matou matua tuupuna; kei

*runga katoa i te whenua nei korerongia atu ki te
tangata na e Peini.*

[*Subtitled*: The bathing waters, the caves, that house,
the remains of our ancestors are all part of this land.
Explain it to the man, Baines].

STEWART (*Muttering to* BAINES *across the previous
speech.*): What do they say? Are they selling? Offer the
blankets for half the land.

STEWART *holds up his ten fingers and then two more.*

STEWART: T-w-e-l-v-e.

BAINES: *Te, kaumarua paraikete mo te tahi hāwhe o te
whenua nei.* [He'll give you twelve blankets for half
the land.]

The MAORIS *look carefully at the quality of the blankets,
noting the depth of the weave and the strength of the
wool. They shake their heads as they discuss them.*

STEWART (*Quietly to* BAINES.): What about the guns?

BAINES: *Kei te hiahia pu koutou.*

[He offers guns too.]

MAORI NEGOTIATOR: *Kahore atu he kororo. Kahore
matou Kote hoko whenua. Engari mo te poaka ae.*
[*Subtitled*: No more talk, we won't sell the land. We
will trade you pigs, that is all.]

He messes up the pattern of twigs as he speaks.

ANGRY MAORI (*Angrily to the* NEGOTIATOR.): *He aha te
pononga o te whenua pena kahore he pu hei pupuri?*
[*Subtitled*: What is the point of owning our land if we
have no guns to hold it?]

The MAORI NEGOTIATOR *gets up to leave, as do the
others.* STEWART *snatches back his blankets and sulkily
shakes them out to fold.*

BAINES: *E hoa ma, haria atu ra taku kia Nihe.*

[Give my regards to Chief Nihe.]

MAORI NEGOTIATOR (*Others join in.*): *Ae ra! Kia Ora! Kia Ora! Te Peini.*

[Yes indeed! Thank you. Thank you, Peini.]

73. EXT. BUSH AT NEW BOUNDARY MARKERS. DAY.
BAINES *and* STEWART *walk through the bush,* STEWART *laden down with his blankets, red-faced and irritable.*
STEWART: What do they want it for? They don't cultivate it, burn it back, anything. How do they even know it's theirs . . .?

BAINES *stops as he comes to a freshly placed fence post.* STEWART *winds down his complaints, watching* BAINES *anxiously.* BAINES *walks down to the next one, he touches the freshly split post.*
STEWART (*Tentatively.*): I thought I might as well mark it out.

BAINES: Yes, why not?
STEWART: Ada says you're doing well with the piano?
BAINES: Oh yes, not bad. (*Walking on to the next post.*) You've been working hard.
STEWART: Not like mastering the ivories, is it?
BAINES *keeps walking from post to post.*
STEWART: I'll have to come and hear you play. Do you sing as well? I like songs. What do you play?
BAINES: Nothing just yet.
STEWART: No. Well, I suppose it takes time. So, what, you just do scales, do you?

74. EXT. STEWART'S VEGETABLE PATCH. DAY.
ADA *has cut a good-sized cabbage in the vegetable patch. She throws it to* FLORA, *who misses, dropping it in a pool of mud, splattering her face and dress.* ADA *smiles and* FLORA, *who was about to cry, gives the cabbage a big*

football boot towards her mother. ADA's *mouth falls open, but then she too kicks it and they begin to dribble the mud-caked cabbage towards the hut, all the time signing playful insults. Into this arrives* STEWART.

STEWART: Baines can't play a damn thing. Is that right, he
    can't play a thing?

    We're going to lose that land, the way he was
    carrying on over it.

    Is he musical? You've got to teach him a song.
    Something simple.

FLORA *has her foot on the cabbage, she nudges it off behind her. It rolls down the hill.* STEWART *can't help but notice.*

STEWART: What's that?

He follows the cabbage down the hill, where he scrapes some of the mud off.

    This thing's been knocked to pieces.

75. INT./EXT. BAINES'S HUT. DAY.

FLORA *is seen through* BAINES's *window. Inside,* ADA *as ever charts her progress on the black keys, eleven. She turns to* BAINES *for instructions.* BAINES *is not himself, he is sulky and distant.*

BAINES: Do what you like. Play what you like.

ADA *is perplexed by this turn about of behaviour. A little uncertainly, she sets about her playing. After a little she too turns to see what* BAINES *is doing. He's not there. She is surprised, then anxious, as she fears the deal may be off when there are now so few keys to go. She starts to play again, but her anxieties prove too great. She stops and listens. She looks out of the window, to where* FLORA *is mucking about in the yard. She walks to his bedroom, listens, then opens the door.* BAINES *stands naked, looking at her.* ADA *is taken aback.*

71

BAINES: I want to lie together without clothes on. How
    many would that be?

ADA *holds up ten fingers – an impossibly high number of
keys.*

BAINES *nods.*

ADA *is surprised; she didn't expect him to agree.* ADA
checks again, holding up her hands.

BAINES: Yes, ten keys.

*Hesitantly, she starts to undress. She lies on her petticoat,
having deemed the bed too dirty.* BAINES *lies, very still, on
top of her. A scraping sound is heard.*

76. EXT./INT. BAINES'S HUT. DAY.

FLORA *is outside walking along sticks and logs trying to
make sure she never puts her foot on the ground. She
looks over at the house, suddenly aware that the piano
playing has stopped again. She investigates the mystery,
peeping through the various cracks and holes in the loosely
built hut. Her vision is always only parts of bodies, the
venture is one of challenge and curiosity.*

77. EXT. NATIVE PINE FOREST. DAY.

FLORA *and three small* MAORI CHILDREN *play amongst
some native pines. Two* MAORI WOMEN *smoke and chat
nearby. The children rub up and down against the tree
trunks, kissing and hugging them. The game has an edge
of promiscuity to it as they exchange trunks and hug one
tree as a group. Unseen by the children,* STEWART *marches
towards* FLORA. *He pulls her off the tree.*

STEWART: Never behave like that, never, nowhere. You
    are greatly shamed and you have shamed those trunks.

The MAORI WOMEN *keep up an unacknowledged chant.*

MAORI WOMEN: – What o'clock say Mr Stewart?

– *Ge Tupeka?*
  [Got tobacco?]
– Time for puff puff.

78. EXT. NATIVE PINE FOREST. DAY.
With a bucket of dull soapy water FLORA *begins the task
of washing the tree trunks.*

The MAORI WOMEN *laugh and point to their feet,
meaning her to wash them too. Their children are lying in
their laps playing string games.*

79. EXT. NATIVE PINE FOREST. DUSK.
FLORA *is still washing the tree trunk, silhouetted against
the evening sky.* FLORA *is tearful and sorry for herself.
The job has an increased futility as it has begun to rain.*
STEWART *is inspecting her penance. She follows* STEWART
about the trees.
FLORA (*Sulkily.*): I know why Mr Baines can't play the
  piano.
STEWART: You've missed this bit.
FLORA: She never gives him a turn.
STEWART *stops and looks at her.*
  She just plays whatever she pleases, sometimes she
  doesn't play at all.
STEWART *continues through the trees more slowly.*
STEWART: And when is the next lesson?
FLORA: Tomorrow.
FLORA *puts her bucket on her head to protect herself from
the rain.*

80. EXT. PATH TO BAINES'S HUT. DAY.
*The next day is very windy; the tops of trees are thrashed
by fierce gusts of wind and some smaller branches crash to*

the ground. ADA's *long dress and cape flap uncontrollably.*
FLORA's *smaller cape stands out on end. Birds fly in mad,*
wind-battered courses, swooped up then strangely drawn
down.

81. EXT. BAINES'S HUT. DAY.
ADA *and* FLORA *arrive at* BAINES's *place to see the piano*
emerge from the hut carried by six MAORI MEN, *one of*
whom does nothing but walk beside it 'plonking' the keys.
Another group of MAORIS *sit cross-legged on the verandah*
playing draughts. Panicked, ADA *hurries down the hill to*
the hut. FLORA *follows behind.*

82. INT. BAINES'S HUT. DAY.
Inside the hut, HIRA, *the old woman from the bathing*
spot, is smoking her pipe. ADA *enters, distraught, and*
indicates what she has seen. Her face is flushed and
whipped by the wind. She is much more expressive than
normal.
BAINES: I am giving the piano back to you. I've had
    enough.

    The arrangement is making you a whore and me
    wretched.

    I want you to care for me, but you can't.
BAINES *sits down on a chair and prepares to eat,*
somewhat ignoring ADA. ADA *is confused, not quite*
believing the situation. She watches BAINES *for some kind*
of confirmation.
HIRA (*Softly.*): George, can I use this comb?
BAINES *nods.* ADA *is still watching.* HIRA *scrapes the inside*
of her pipe with the comb.
BAINES: It's yours, leave, go on, go!
ADA *is off-balanced by the reversal of attitudes, surprised,*

too, that she doesn't want to go. FLORA *is fast to leave;* ADA *follows to organize and protect her piano on the journey.*

83. EXT. BAINES'S HUT AND BUSH. DAY.
As she climbs out of the small valley surrounding BAINES'*s hut, she stops and walks back to look down at* BAINES *and his hut, in the* exact *same manner that she once looked at her piano from the cliff top above the beach.* BAINES *is throwing the scraps of his meal to his dog; he does not look up.*

84. EXT. PATH TO BAINES'S HUT WITH STEEP HILL. DAY.
STEWART, *on his way to* BAINES, *sees the piano bearers and* ADA *way below him in the bush. He scrambles down a steep slope towards them.*
STEWART (*Still from some distance.*): Stop right there! This isn't yours . . . What are you doing with the piano?
The women exchange looks.
FLORA: He's given it to us.
STEWART (*Out of breath.*): Hah, you're very cunning, Ada, but I've seen through you, I'm not going to lose the land this way. Wait here!
STEWART *is off, pounding on down through the bush.*

85. EXT./INT. BAINES'S HUT/BEDROOM. DAY.
HIRA *is sitting on the front step of* BAINES'*s place, blocking* STEWART'*s easy access.*
HIRA: George sick, he don't wanna see nobody. You got *Tupeka* for the Hira?
STEWART *goes around to a side window in* BAINES'*s bedroom.* BAINES *is sitting on the bed, but lies back as he*

hears STEWART *coming about the side of the house.*
STEWART *opens up the window.*

STEWART: I don't think you should have given up the piano. I will make sure you are properly taught, with music written on to sheets and . . .

BAINES: I don't want to learn.

STEWART: You don't want to learn.

BAINES: No.

STEWART: And what does this do to our bargain? I cannot afford the piano if you mean me to pay.

BAINES: No, no payment. I have given it back. I don't want it.

STEWART: Well, I doubt I want it very much myself.

BAINES: It was more to your wife that I gave it.

STEWART: Well, thank you, I expect she will appreciate it. *He closes the window.*

So that is agreed on?

BAINES *nods.*

HIRA *has wandered silently into* BAINES's *room. She sits on the edge of his bed.*

HIRA: You make BIG mistake, George. In first place you should swap land for wife. Now look, she gone, you no land, no music box, you got nothing.

86. EXT. STEWART'S HUT. DAY.
In the distance a small procession of piano bearers pick their way through the huge ghostly stumps to STEWART's *hut.*

87. EXT./INT. STEWART'S HUT. DAY.
At the door of the hut STEWART *is distributing buttons to the piano bearers. One squats, catching them as they fall. A commotion begins as one of the* MAORIS *snatches the*

whole jar and runs off. Two of them give chase, while the other insist on tobacco.[11]

Inside the hut ADA *has lifted the top of the piano and is peering in while playing to check tune and damage.*
STEWART: Is it all right? Aren't you going to play something?
ADA *pulls up a chair and seats herself at the piano. She rubs her hands and places them lightly on the keys; she turns from habit over her left shoulder where* STEWART *waits, arms crossed. Quickly she removes her hands, stands and gestures* FLORA *to play.* FLORA *proudly takes up the seat; she pulls her lips in trying to control her happiness to play in front of both her mother and* STEWART.
FLORA: What will I play?
She looks to ADA, *who looks back through her, not concentrating.*
STEWART: Play a jig.
FLORA (*To* ADA.): Do I know any jigs?
STEWART: Play a song then . . .
FLORA *starts a song;* ADA *walks past them out of the hut;* STEWART *ignores her exit, moving up to lean on the piano.* ADA *is seen through the hut window wandering amidst the ghostly, blackened trunks.* STEWART's *attention is drawn to* ADA; *he interrupts* FLORA's *singing with a sudden outburst.*
STEWART (*Exasperated.*): Why won't she play it? We have it back, and she just wanders off!
FLORA *stops to watch her mother through the window.*
ADA *looks towards the house as the music stops.*
STEWART: Keep playing!

[11] See notes, p. 129.

Grimly, STEWART *slaps the top of the piano to* FLORA's *playing.*

ADA *continues to walk, her face dark and puzzled. She stops. Her head stiffly, irresistibly, lifts and turns in the direction of* BAINES's *hut. She peers deep into the bush as if attempting to penetrate a puzzle. She blinks and walks on.*

88. INT. STEWART'S KITCHEN. DAY.

The next day ADA *and her piano face each other across the kitchen. A slit of light falls across the piano, highlighting its rosy walnut wood.* ADA's *expression is critical and distant.*

Taking a cloth, she begins to clean and polish the piano. Her finger holds down one of the keys and we glimpse an old inscription on its side, a small heart, A arrow D. Putting the cloth aside, she sits at the piano to begin playing.

She starts with wholehearted feeling, her eyes closed, but before long she is surprised by a moving reflection across the piano and she starts, glancing over her shoulder. She stops and begins again. But once more a reflex has her glance across her left shoulder and she pauses in her playing. Disquieted, she starts again and again she looks away. She stops, confused, unable to go on, unable to get up, one hand on the lid and one on the piano keys.

89. EXT. PATH TO BAINES'S HUT. DAY.

ADA, *carrying her cape and bonnet, hurries along the narrow bush path to* BAINES's *hut;* FLORA *has a fist of her skirt and is pulling back.* ADA *turns on* FLORA *and snatches the skirt out of the girl's hand.* ADA *signs to her and continues on.*

FLORA: Why? Why can't I?

ADA *signs again.*

FLORA (*Crossing her arms.*): I shan't practise and I
    DON'T CARE!

But ADA *does not wait to listen.* FLORA *walks back
through the bush muttering childish expletives to herself.*
STEWART *and his two* MAORI HELPERS *come out of the
bush towards her.* FLORA *squeals with fright.*

STEWART (*Looking up the hill.*): Where's your mother?
    Where has she gone?

FLORA *pauses, petulant and grumpy.*

FLORA: To HELL!

FLORA *races off as fast as she can, enlivened by her
wickedness.*

STEWART *clambers back up the path. He just glimpses the
distant figure of* ADA *nervously turning, her skirts flying as
she hurries up the bush path. The wind bothers the tops of
the trees, setting them groaning, rubbing their branches
against each other.*

90. INT. BAINES'S HUT. DAY.

ADA *enters* BAINES'*s hut; she is breathless, announcing her
presence by simply being there, standing there.* BAINES
comes through from the bedroom. Seeing ADA *he is aloof,
suspicious, and his blinking becomes pronounced.*

BAINES: So what brings you here? Did you leave
    something? I have not found anything.

ADA *does not respond; finally she looks at* BAINES *and her
look has a vulnerability and frankness that takes him off
guard.*

    Does he know something?

ADA *shakes her head.*

    The piano is not harmed? It arrived safely? Would you
    like to sit? I am going to sit.

ADA *does not sit. She stands immobilized.* BAINES *attempts to maintain his casual charade, he pours a cup of tea.*

He turns to her, about to speak, but stops, unmanned by a new fragility to her strength. He blinks rapidly.

BAINES: Ada, I am unhappy because I want you, because my mind has seized on you and thinks of nothing else. This is how I suffer. I am sick with longing. I don't eat, I don't sleep. If you do not want me, if you have come with no feeling for me, then go!

BAINES *walks roughly towards the door and opens it, his softness turned suddenly cruel.*

Go! Go NOW! Leave!

ADA *is stung by his change of tune; she takes a step towards him and, eyes filling with tears of anger, hits him hard across the face.* BAINES's *nose begins to bleed yet his face slowly lights up as if she has spoken words of love.* ADA *is flushed, shocked; the two face each other at this very moment profoundly aware of each other, profoundly equal. With each new breath, with every moment that their eyes remain locked together, the promise of intimacy is confirmed and reconfirmed and detailed until, like sleepwalkers who do not know how they came to wake where they did, they are standing next to each other and beginning to kiss each other, the lips, the cheeks, the nose. There is nothing practised about their tenderness, only their feelings and emotions guide their instincts.* BAINES's *face crumples with the exquisite pain of his pleasure;* ADA *cradles his head to her chest.* BAINES *struggles through her dress, anxious to touch her skin.*

91. EXT. INT. BAINES'S HUT. DAY.
Outside, STEWART *surveys the hut suspiciously.* BAINES's *dog growls as he climbs on to the small verandah.*

Carefully, STEWART *peers through some loosely slatted boards. There are sounds inside which are worrying him. By standing on the seat he has found a spyhole where he can see* ADA *and* BAINES *kissing, undressing.*

He reels back, angry, but just as we might expect him to burst through, he steps up to look again; the fatal second look, the look for curiosity. He watches BAINES, *bare-chested, undressing* ADA; *her buttons burst,* ADA *laughs,* BAINES *touches her under her skirts – anywhere – he takes himself under her dress, pulling down her stockings.* STEWART *watches, stepping down to peer lower as* BAINES *buries into* ADA's *skirt. He does not seem to notice the dog licking his hand. Suddenly he pulls his hand away and looks at it, wet with dog saliva; he wipes it on the boards and continues watching as if mesmerized.*

92. INT. BAINES'S BEDROOM. DAY.
Inside BAINES's *small bedroom the raw dark boards contrast with the softness, whiteness, of* BAINES's *and* ADA's *bodies. The long black strands of* ADA's *hair stick to her cheek and wrap around her neck. Her face is flushed and her eyes are bright.* BAINES *rolls his face across her chest, gently, slowly, savouring the flavour of her body. Drunkenly they continue their sex, softly, slowly.* ADA's *breaths turn to low murmurs; these small sounds are extraordinarily moving to* BAINES, *whose face swoons with joy.*
BAINES: What? . . . What? . . . Whisper . . .!

93. INT. BAINES'S BEDROOM AND UNDER THE HOUSE. DAY.
As ADA *dresses,* BAINES *sits on his bed watching. He is unhappy, thoughtful.*

BAINES: Now you are going I am miserable, why is that?
(*He catches her hand and draws her to him.*) Ada, I
need to know, what will you do? Will you come
again?

ADA *is distracted, collecting her buttons from the floor,
worried by the time that has passed, concerned to dress
and return.*

The camera cranes down and down to find STEWART
*wedged under the loose wooden floor slats. He cannot
hear clearly, but* ADA's *hand reaching for each button is
only inches away. One falls through a slat on to*
STEWART's *neck and on down his shirt collar. As she
stands he rolls out.*

BAINES: Wait! I don't know what you're thinking. (*Gently,
teasingly.*) Does this mean something to you? Hey?
(*Stroking a strand of hair behind her ear.*) I already
miss you. Ada, do you love me?

ADA *considers this question. Clearly she doesn't know, the
question is more complex to her than to him; then, as if by
way of answer, she kisses him strongly and sexually.*

BAINES *pulls away, confused.* ADA *finishes dressing.*

BAINES *comes up behind her to help with the buttons.*

BAINES (*Anxiously.*): Come tomorrow. If you are serious,
come tomorrow.

ADA *turns and kisses him passionately, with the new-born
enthusiasm of someone who has just discovered their
appetite for sex. Then, as quickly as she began, she takes
her hood and cape and goes to leave.*

BAINES: Tomorrow?

She nods and is gone.

94. INT. STEWART'S HUT/ADA'S BEDROOM. NIGHT.
FLORA *and* ADA *are both in their white nightgowns.*

FLORA *stands behind* ADA *on a chair trying to sort out the knots that have matted at the back of* ADA's *head.* ADA *shakes her head from side to side playfully, making the difficult job impossible.*

FLORA: Stay still! It's the very worst knots.

FLORA *tries to hold her mother's head still, but* ADA's *high spirits are unstoppable and her hair flies out from side to side, flicking* FLORA *in the face.*

FLORA: Mama, STOP IT!

FLORA *starts to giggle, and retaliates, flinging her own hair from side to side. The two women are twirling in the small bedroom, their hair flying about them;* FLORA *is shrieking with the fun, then stops dizzy and sick.* ADA *continues flicking* FLORA *as she twirls.*

FLORA: Stop it! I feel sick!

But ADA *doesn't stop; her dark hair whirls about her as, giddy and disorientated, she knocks against the walls.*

95. INT. STEWART'S HUT. NIGHT.
Next door, STEWART *sits on his bed listening, his hair wet and neatly combed. He has a journal of pressed botanical specimens beside him. Hearing* FLORA *squealing, he goes to the kitchen and, standing back in the shadows, watches* ADA's *frenetic whirling through the part-open door.*

96. INT. STEWART'S HUT/ADA'S BEDROOM. DAWN.
Daylight floods the room as ADA *secures the pins at the back of her hair.*

97. EXT. PATH TO BAINES'S HUT. DAY.
(Music builds up throughout.) The sky is dark and the wind is ballooning ADA's *cape, wrapping it up high around her. The tree tops are swaying furiously. Inside the*

bush it is dark, and ADA *hurries up through the path. She is out of breath, and glancing behind her as if to guard against followers, when directly in front of her* STEWART *steps out on to the path.* ADA *stops short. The look on his face is unlike any expression she has yet seen. His eyes do not look at her but all about her in a way more animal than human. She lowers her eyes and, calling his bluff, walks steadily past him. But* STEWART *takes her arm and, spinning her back, pulls her close and, blind to all protest, kisses her.* ADA *struggles furiously. His grip falters and she steps back, staring at him, then runs off down the hill, but* STEWART *is on top of her, clasping her skirts, pulling her towards him hand over hand; she slips and falls to the ground.* STEWART *is upon her, lifting her dress, touching her legs;* ADA *goes quite still, which throws* STEWART *long enough for her to scramble away. Yet again* STEWART *catches her and again they roll on the ground,* STEWART *touching and kissing her,* ADA *turning herself this way and that to avoid it. There is a cat and mouse quality to their mute struggle, finally broken by* FLORA *calling up the path, distraught and in tears, her angel wings twisted about her waist.*

FLORA (*Top of her lungs.*): Mama! Mama! They are
    playing your piano!

STEWART *allows* ADA *to get up and the two women go back down the path towards home. Distant sound of the piano keys thumping.*

98. INT. STEWART'S HUT. DAY.
At the piano and with solemn dignity sits a MAORI
WOMAN. *She is wearing a top hat and a long black dress; beside her stands the* MAORI *who absconded with the buttons, most of which he has attached to his jacket. She*

plays loudly with two closed fists; her companion listens
gravely, placidly, blinking at the crashes; two others listen
from the doorway, one with his hands over his head.

99. INT./EXT. STEWART'S HUT. DAY.
FLORA *and* ADA *stand in the hut while fierce hammering*
can be heard outside. STEWART *is boarding over the*
windows, barricading them in. FLORA *joins in the spirit of*
the exercise, gaily pointing out any slats STEWART *has*
missed.
FLORA: Here, Papa!
ADA'*s face pales in the diminishing light. Exasperated by*
the threatened incarceration, she shakes her head with
anguish and, moving to the piano, lifts the lid and plays
several bars brutally and strongly. She passes on to the
bedroom, where she picks up the small hand mirror and
looks at her face, puckered with frustration. She touches
her face and neck tenderly, then throws herself on the bed,
face to the wall, her hands over her ears.
  FLORA *stands over her mother.*
FLORA: You shouldn't have gone up there, should you? I
    don't like it and nor does Papa. Mama, we can play
    cards together.
ADA *rolls over; her eyes closed, she pushes her face and*
body against the mattress. The movement is sensual and
removed. FLORA *stops dealing the cards on to the bed and*
watches her mother, puzzled.

100. INT. STEWART'S HUT. NIGHT.
It is night and ADA *is walking in the dark, ghostly in her*
white nightgown. She sits at her piano and begins to play,
loudly and strongly. Her hair is loose and she seems half-
asleep. FLORA *and* STEWART *wake to the loud playing and*

fumble their way to the kitchen. STEWART *carries a lit candle.* ADA *continues her playing.*

FLORA *passes a hand in front of* ADA's *face.*

FLORA: She is asleep, look.

One night she was found in her nightgown on the road to London. Grandpa said her feet were cut and bleeding so badly she couldn't walk for a week.

The two watch ADA, *mesmerized by her compulsive playing.*[12]

101. EXT. STREAM NEAR STEWART'S HUT. DAY.

STEWART *stands guard while* ADA *and* FLORA *wash their clothes in the stream.* FLORA *is taking the lead, soaping up the clothes; she passes the garments to her mother to rinse.* ADA *is distracted and, as she takes the clothes, she just as soon lets them go and they float off down the stream past* STEWART *who tries to catch them but can't. Two* MAORI BOYS *continue the chase, enjoying the fun, thinking it a great adventure.*

STEWART: You are letting the clothes float off . . . They are floating off!

ADA *stares off into the distance, rocking lightly back and forth as she crouches on a stone. Her dress, unhitched, floats down the stream behind her.*

FLORA: Mama! Look out!

FLORA *wades across to grasp yet another garment* ADA *has let drift off.*

102. EXT. STEWART'S HUT. DAY.

On the way back to the barricaded hut FLORA *swings between* ADA *and* STEWART.

[12] See notes, p. 130.

FLORA: One, two, three . . . One, two, three . . .
ADA *glances around at the bush.* FLORA *beams, enjoying
the feeling of having a family of which she is now the
boss. The two women go ahead into the hut which*
STEWART *shuts and secures with a beam.*

103. INT. STEWART'S HUT/ADA'S BEDROOM. NIGHT.
It is night. ADA *is tossing in the small bed beside* FLORA,
*her hair wound across her face; she makes low moaning
sounds as she pushes her face and body up against the
sleeping* FLORA. *Her movement and moans increase until
she wakes suddenly, sitting bolt upright.*

104. INT. STEWART'S KITCHEN AND BEDROOM. NIGHT.
ADA *walks through the kitchen, small slithers of moonlight
lighting her path. She walks past the piano into*
STEWART's *room; he has gone to sleep with his candle still
alight.* ADA *looks, then slowly her hand hovers above him
before lightly touching his face. His eyes open, he looks
towards* ADA, *anxious and surprised, but as* ADA
*continues, his reserve breaks and he is captive to his own
sensations. She pulls down the sheet and strokes his neck,
shoulders, chest; he reaches out towards her.*
STEWART: Ada!
But ADA *scowls and pulls away roughly;* STEWART *lies
back, anxious not to break the spell, and when he is still*
ADA *continues to caress his chest. His eyes well with tears
and he looks up into her face like a child after a bad
dream, fearful and trusting.* ADA *continues like a nurse
spreading ointment on a wound; tenderly and attentively
she strokes down towards his belly.* STEWART's *skin goose
bumps and he shudders. He puts his hand on hers to still
it; she slides hers out and continues stroking. He looks at*

89

her pleadingly, and childlike she stops and kisses the soft skin of his belly. STEWART *groans, clutching the mattress.* ADA *seems removed from* STEWART *as if she has a separate curiosity of her own.*

105. INT. STEWART'S KITCHEN. DAY.
Next day AUNT MORAG *stands turning and turning about in* STEWART'*s small darkened house.* FLORA *and* ADA *sit quietly together.*

AUNT MORAG: Ohhh, it's so dark, it's like a dank cave.
NESSIE: Yes, like a cave.
AUNT MORAG: Ohh no, it makes my skin creep!
STEWART *comes into the house with some logs;* AUNT MORAG *follows him across to the fire.*

AUNT MORAG: Alisdair, is it because of our play? Have the natives aggressed you?
She continues, following him to the door.

   I have to say you have done the wrong thing here, you see you have put the latch on the outside. When you close the door (*and she closes it*) it will be the Maoris that lock you in, you see? With the latch on that side you are quite trapped.
NESSIE: (*Nodding her head in imitation.*): . . . you are quite trapped.
AUNT MORAG *walks inside and continues to the table where her basket full of clothes and packets of food has been left. She lifts it from the table and begins to spread the cloth.*

AUNT MORAG: We have just come from George Baines and they have taken him over. It is no wonder he is leaving, he has got in too deep with the natives. They sit on his floor as proud as kings, but without a shred of manners.

90

NESSIE (*In unison*): . . . without a shred of manners.

NESSIE *and* AUNT MORAG *are unpacking parcels of cakes and biscuits, putting them on plates about the table.*

AUNT MORAG: He is quite altered, as if they had been trying some native witchcraft on him. Well, tomorrow or the day after he will be gone.

STEWART: Baines is packing up?

AUNT MORAG: Well, he has *nothing* to pack, but he is leaving. And it is just as well; Nessie has foolishly grown an affection for him . . . we have had some tears . . .

At this mention, NESSIE's *face crumples and tears again begin to flow.*

AUNT MORAG (*Very firmly.*): STOP IT! STOP!

NESSIE, *remarkably, obeys, blinking her face back to shape.*

ADA *attempts to disguise her agitation; she moves to the piano and strokes it; she begins to play.*

AUNT MORAG: I am quite frightened of the way back, we must leave in good light. Will we be safe?

STEWART (*Wanting them gone.*): If you leave soon, yes, I am sure of it.

STEWART *and* MORAG *watch* ADA *at the piano. Her playing develops until she is fully absorbed.* AUNT MORAG *is intrigued despite herself.*

106. EXT. BUSH ROAD TO MISSION. DAY.

On the edge of the bush beside the dirt road to town

AUNT MORAG *attempts a discreet toilet stop.* NESSIE *keeps guard, holding up the cape, while one of their* MAORI *charges holds up another.*

AUNT MORAG: You know, I am thinking of the piano. She does not play the piano as we do, Nessie.

The cape begins to droop as NESSIE *listens.*

> UP! UP! No, she is a strange creature and her playing is strange, like a mood that passes into you. You cannot teach that, Nessie, one may like to learn, but that could not be taught.

NESSIE *again lets the cape droop.*

> UP! Your playing is plain and true and that is what I like. To have a sound creep inside you is not all pleasant . . .

A fluttering sound in the bush.

> . . . What is that?

NESSIE (*Frightened.*): Ohhhhhh!

MARY/HENI (*Slow, relaxed.*): A pid-geon, Auntie.

The party finish and hurry, a little spooked, on the road to town.

107. INT. STEWART'S ROOM. NIGHT.

It is night. ADA *enters the room;* STEWART *looks at her shyly.*

STEWART: I've been hoping you would come.

ADA *strokes his brow.* STEWART *closes his eyes, breathing heavily, relieved.* ADA *strokes the nape of his neck and on down his back.* STEWART's *face puckers, his eyes fill with tears. She strokes so softly, the tenderness is shocking to him. Gently she pulls his under-garments down, exposing his buttocks.* STEWART *grabs nervously at them, hauling them up with his hands.* ADA *unclenches his fist and once more, slowly, pulls them down. She begins to stroke his buttocks.* STEWART *is painfully eroticized, painfully vulnerable; he begins to weep, the intimacy and softness unmans him and he is helpless.* STEWART *sits up, hunching over himself, retreating.*

STEWART: I want to touch you. Why can't I touch you?

Do you like me?

Slowly he raises his head to look at ADA. *She looks back, moved by his helplessness, but distanced, as if it has nothing to do with her.*

Do you?

ADA *does not respond.* STEWART *slumps into disappointment and despair.*

Why? Why not?!

108. INT. STEWART'S KITCHEN. DAY.

The next morning, ADA, FLORA *and* STEWART *sit together in the small dark hut.* FLORA *preens a miniature landscape of moss and tiny branches, all piled on a dinner plate. A slit of sunlight falling across the top small branches gives it a magical glow.* FLORA's *small dirty fingers push in another 'tree'; she looks up happily.*

FLORA: This is going to be Adam's tree and then I'm going
    to make a serpent to live here, with a very long
    tongue. (*She pokes her tongue out and waggles it.*)

STEWART *reads; he glances at* ADA *who is glum and
    lifeless.*

109. INT. STEWART'S HUT. DAY.

ADA *and* FLORA *wake to sunlight streaming in on their faces, more and more of it as* STEWART *rips the boards from the windows.* FLORA *runs about in nightgown and boots, happy to be in the sunlight.* ADA *winds her hair into a bun.* STEWART *walks inside; he packs food and fencing equipment.*

STEWART (*Clears his throat.*): We must both get on. I have
    decided to trust you to stay here. You will not see
    Baines?

ADA *nods.*

Good, good. Perhaps with more trying you will
come to like me?

110. EXT. STEWART'S HUT. DAY.
ADA *hangs out washing, restlessly scanning the bushline. A
tiny* STEWART *walks along the crest of the hill, eventually
dropping out of sight.*

111. INT. STEWART'S HUT. DAY.
Inside the hut ADA *is pacing, anguished and frustrated.
Impulsively she picks up a knife from the kitchen table,
opens the back of the piano and cuts one of the keys
loose. Carefully she engraves on the side in Victorian
handscript:*
DEAR GEORGE, YOU HAVE MY HEART,
ADA McGRATH.

112. EXT. STEWART'S HUT. DAY.
Under the sheets FLORA *has constructed a dolls' clothes
line on which she hangs small strips of cloth.* ADA *hands
her the key, wrapped and tied in white cotton.* ADA *signs.
Her black shadow behind the sheet recalls the macabre
play.*
FLORA: No!
*The little girl continues defiantly with her miniature
washing.* ADA *rips the washing line up and flings it aside.*
FLORA *is shocked, stunned. She takes the key and, walking
off, she turns and shouts.*
FLORA: We're not supposed to visit him!
ADA *signals:* 'GO!'

113. EXT. PATH TO BAINES'S HUT AT FENCE. DAY.
At the junction of the path to BAINES's *hut is the*

beginning of STEWART's *boundary fence. At this place*
FLORA *has paused. She looks back to see if her mother is*
watching; she's not. FLORA *turns sharply right so that she*
now follows alongside STEWART's *boundary fence and*
away from BAINES's *hut.*

114. EXT. HILLS WITH FENCE. DAY.
The fence appears and disappears behind hills. FLORA *too*
dips behind hills to reappear on the other side. She sings a
brisk song to herself:
FLORA: The grand old Duke of York. He had ten
thousand men (*etc.*)

115. EXT. VALLEY WITH FOXGLOVES AND FENCE. DAY.
Flora pauses in one of the valleys, stilled by clumps of tall,
mauve foxglove.

116. EXT. INCOMPLETE FENCE ON HILL. DAY.
The fence line seems endless as the tired FLORA *trudges up*
yet another hill, but from there she can see where the fence
finishes, half-way up the crest of the next hill, and at this
point is STEWART, *driving in a new fence post. He is*
watched by the BUTTON MAN *and his friend, who squat*
passing a pipe between themselves. The BUTTON MAN
strums tirelessly on his buttons.
FLORA: Mama wanted me to give this to Mr Baines.
She holds out the cotton-covered piano key. STEWART
looks up.
    I thought maybe it was not a proper thing to do.
STEWART *keeps working, hammering the post into the*
earth.
    Shall I open it?
STEWART: No!!

He stops and takes the key, suspicious and uncomfortable.
He slowly unwraps it and, turning it over, reads it.
Squeezing the key in his fist, STEWART *staggers off in a*
daze. He returns, picks up his open pack, spilling the nails.
Finally he drops the pack and the key, and leaves with
only his axe. FLORA *follows, confused. The* MAORIS *waste*
no time investigating the booty. The BUTTON MAN *presses*
the piano key repeatedly.
BUTTON MAN: *Kaare e Waiata! Kaare e Waiata!*

[*Subtitled*: No sing, no sing]

117. EXT. STEWART'S HUT. DAY.
STEWART *bursts into the hut; his wet hair is splattered*
against his forehead, his face is white. ADA *looks up from*
her book, moving her hands from the table. STEWART
swings his axe hard. It slices into the table, splitting a
section off her book. ADA *pushes her chair back.*
STEWART (*Exasperated.*): Why? WHY? I trusted you!
He pulls the axe out of the table and swings it at the
piano.

WHY?
ADA *runs forward to restrain him, but it sinks deep into*
the wood. The struck piano lets out a strange resonant
moan.

I trusted you, do you hear? I trusted you. I could love
you.
He takes her by the wrist.

Why do you do this? Why do you make me hurt you?
Do you hear? Why have you done it? We could be
happy.
STEWART *shakes her violently.*

You have made me angry. SPEAK!

119. EXT. STEWART'S HUT AND WOODCHOP. DAY.

He pulls out of the hut, past the now terrified FLORA.

> You shall answer for this. Speak or not you shall
> answer for it!

*He drags her out through the mud, towards the
woodchop. It is raining hard.*

ADA *sees where they are headed and suddenly she is
very scared. She bucks and struggles, but* STEWART *is
infinitely stronger. At the woodchop she breaks free and
crawls away through the woodchips and mud. But, axe in
hand, he grasps her by the neck of her dress, then her hair,
and pulls her backwards towards the cutting block. There,
he takes her right hand and holds it in place with his boot,
so that only* ADA's *index finger shows.* ADA's *head is held
twisted between the woodchop and* STEWART's *leg.*

STEWART (*Anguished.*): Do you love him? Do you?! Is it
> him you love?

ADA *blinks, rigid with fear. The rain is driving down.*

FLORA: No, she says, NOOOOOO!!!

The axe falls. ADA's *face buckles in pain. Blood squirts on
to* FLORA's *white pinafore, her angel wings are splattered
in mud.*

FLORA (*Screaming.*): Mother!!

ADA *stands. She looks faint; her finger is pulsing blood,
she shakes her hand, then, seeing the blood, she puts it
behind her back, shocked. She watches* FLORA, *concerned
and confused. Uncontrollably, her whole body starts to
shake and as if by reflex* ADA *begins to walk.* FLORA *trots
parallel to her.*

FLORA: Mama!

ADA *keeps walking blindly, as if her being depended on it.
Her face is ashen, her eyes fearful as she walks, unseeing,
straight into a large tree stump. She sinks into the mud.*

STEWART *wraps the finger in a white handkerchief and gives it to* FLORA, *who backs away from him, terrified.*
FLORA (*Quietly.*): Mama.
STEWART: Take this to Baines. Tell him if he ever tries to see her again I'll take off another and another and another!
The figures seem tiny amidst the rain-drenched skeleton forest.

120. EXT. MAORI PA. DAY.
BAINES, *his horse and* HIRA *stand at the entrance to the Maori Pa. The Pa stands on the edge of a mangroved river flat and several canoes are pulled up on the flat. The Pa is long established, broken down and repaired. Inside the Pa entrance a* KUIA *is performing the ritual welcome.*
KUIA (*Chanting.*): *Arahingia mai ra to tatou rangatira e Hira. He tangata whai whakaaro kia taua ki te. Maori Haere mai ra! Haere mai, Haere mai!*
[Bring forth our reverend friend, Hira. He's always had a warm feeling for us Maori people. Welcome! Welcome! Thrice Welcome!]

121. EXT. MAORI PA. DAY.
The formal farewells are over and HIRA *and* BAINES *finish shaking hands and pressing noses with her people*
HIRA *holds his arms, she is sad and tearful. He places his hat on her head affectionately and slips her a much appreciated tin of tobacco.*
HIRA: *Peini,* I miss you, you are human like us. The *pakeha* man, they have no heart, they think only of land.
A soft rain begins to fall. BAINES *and* HIRA *make their way past the Meeting House and the low sleeping houses to the Pa entrance where his horse waits.*

HIRA: I worry for us, *Peini*. *Pakeha* cunning like wind,
    KNOCK you over, yet you not see it. Some they say,
    'How can *pakeha* get our land if we won't sell it?'
*A crowd of children run beside them, dogs scurry off and
pigs are kicked out of the way, their owners protesting
loudly. Some hold mats over their heads to protect
themselves from the rain, one has a battered umbrella.*
HIRA: They wrong, *Peini*. Today our enamee he sell some
    land for heapah guns. Now, we too buy guns. We
    must sell our land to fight for our land.
BAINES *mounts his heavily laden horse. The* BUTTON MAN
*pushes forward to say farewell, but is abruptly shoved
aside, evidently unpopular with the others.* BAINES *glances
over and sees the piano key the man has fashioned into an
earring.*
HIRA: I worried, *Peini*. Whas gonna happen you, you go
    home, but where we go? We got nowhere to go.
HIRA'*s voice rises angrily as* BAINES *lets go of her arm and
rides through the group towards the* BUTTON MAN. *He
takes the piano key in his hand; the* BUTTON MAN *pulls
back.*
BUTTON MAN: It is mine. I found it.
BAINES *turns it over and finds the writing on it.*
BAINES (*Urgently.*): *Homai ki au.*
    [*Subtitled*: I want this.]
BUTTON MAN (*Sulky.*): *Norr! Naaku.* Is mine. Me find it.
BAINES: *He aha to hiahia?* Ask for it? Tobacco?
    [*Subtitled*: What do you want?]
HIRA (*Still angry.*): Gun, ask for his gun!
The BUTTON MAN *rubs his nail up and down his buttons
while he considers what he will have.*
OTHERS: – *Nga rarahe*
    [The glasses]

– *Wana Putu*
– *Te whitiki, gettem ehoa!*
[The belt]

122. EXT. MAORI PA. DAY.
Outside the Pa *walls near the* kumera *gardens,* HIRA *holds*
BAINES's *saddle bags. It is raining hard as he rides out,*
hatless, shoeless and gunless, but clutching to his chest
ADA's *engraved key.*
HIRA: Go, *Peini . . . Haere atu e Peini.*
BAINES: I'll be back.

123. EXT. SCHOOL. DAY.
BAINES *crosses through the pony paddock of the one-room*
colonial school house. He has a piece of flax knotted
around his waist to hold up his trousers. The sky is
beginning to clear. In the paddock are five very shabby
looking rides: one huge old wagon horse, built to carry a
whole family, down to a tiny, sour-looking Shetland.
BAINES *listens at the schoolroom wall, where lots of little*
voices recite their times tables.

124. INT. SCHOOLROOM. DAY.
He peeps through a hole in the wall at little legs under
tables.

125. EXT. SCHOOL. DAY.
It is playtime and a whole bunch of straggly children rush
out of the schoolroom. The girls have long, stained, once
white pinafores and everyone wears boots that seem too
big, except the little boy who has the front cut off his
boots so his toes can hang out.

   Four little girls play a sedate game of skip rope, using a

*bush vine. The boys and some of the wilder girls play Bull-
Rush.*

126. EXT. GENTLE STREAM. DAY.
*One little girl of about 7 goes off with a book to sit by a
little stream.* BAINES *follows and sits beside her.*
BAINES: Can you read?
The little girl immediately closes the book and walks off.
    *The girl keeps walking, before she turns about to watch
him from a safe distance.*
    Another little girl drops down from a tree.
TREE GIRL: I can.
BAINES: You can read? (*She is very small.*)
TREE GIRL: Yes . . . lots of things.
The skipping group of girls joins them.
BIG SISTER: She can't read, she's my sister, I ought to
    know.
        Are those sweets?
TREE GIRL: I can read!
BIG SISTER: She can't.
BAINES *holds out the packet to the little girl.*
BIG SISTER: Don't give her one.
BAINES *does anyway.*
BIG SISTER: She can't read.
*The little girl throws the lolly paper away, which one of
the other girls picks up and sniffs; she hands it to the
others.*
    Mmm, caramels.
BAINES: Can you read?
He holds out the piano key. BIG SISTER *takes it with great
authority, her friends crowd behind her. She frowns at the
writing. She turns it over.*
BIG SISTER: Running writing, we haven't done that yet.

107

READING GIRL 1: Myrtle can read it, her mother taught her.

The key is snatched from BIG SISTER *and given to* MYRTLE, *the girl with the book. The others crowd around.*

MYRTLE (*Frowning.*): D e a r G e o r g e . . .

The children look over at BAINES *to see if this is right so far.*

Y o u (*In unison.*) . . . have . . .

BIG SISTER: That's 'my'.

MYRTLE: It's not an 'M'.

BIG SISTER: Yes it is.

MYRTLE AND BIG SISTER: Dear – George – you – have – my –

MYRTLE: – heart? (*She pulls a face as if it doesn't make sense.*) Ada McGrath.

BIG SISTER: It doesn't make sense.

The little girls all read it again together. MYRTLE *turns the key over matter of factly to see if there is more writing.*

MYRTLE: That's all . . .

They all look up at him.

BAINES: Say it again, just you.

Everyone turns and listens to MYRTLE.

MYRTLE: Dear George you have my heart, Ada McGrath.

She gives a little 'Is that all?' gesture.

BAINES: You say it. (*He points to* BIG SISTER, *who has a deep voice.*)

BIG SISTER: Dear George you have my heart, Ada McGrath.

Another little girl spontaneously recites the message. And so does another. Through all this BAINES *keeps his head down, shaking it in disbelief and shy happiness. He starts to laugh with relief and pleasure. The little girls think it is*

something funny in the line and continue to repeat it,
which each time appears to give BAINES *fresh pleasure.*
Meanwhile the smallest of the girls is quietly helping
herself to the sweets.

127. EXT. STEWART'S HUT. DAY.
The figures of STEWART, *his* AUNT *and* NESSIE *are tiny as*
they struggle to carry ADA *through the white-stumped*
marsh in the rain.

128. INT. STEWART'S HUT/ADA'S ROOM. DAY.
NESSIE *and* AUNT MORAG *are removing* ADA's *wet clothes,*
cutting through her sleeve with scissors.
AUNT MORAG (*Distressed.*): Oh dear . . . what an
     accident. And she had wood enough . . . If she doesn't
     die of blood loss, we'll lose her to pneumonia. HOT
     WATER! The mud is everywhere!
NESSIE (*Sobbing.*): Oh, the poor thing . . . ohhh dear . . .
STEWART *brings the hot water into the bedroom. He is*
subdued, anxious, staring on hopelessly.
AUNT MORAG (*Pushing him out.*): Now off you go, that
     glum staring will cure no one.
STEWART *leaves, closing the door.* AUNT MORAG
continues to clean and attend ADA's *wound while* NESSIE
tears sheets into bandage-width strips. ADA *is semi-*
conscious, her eyelids flutter and close, while her lips
move, as if to speak.
AUNT MORAG: Look at these lips . . . What a story they
     try to tell.
NESSIE *combs her hair out with great care and tenderness.*
ADA's *body is shivering.* NESSIE *looks across at* MORAG.
NESSIE: Might I put a blanket on? She is quite cooled
     down.

AUNT MORAG: Yes, very well, very well.

NESSIE *pulls the cover over her. The two older women look at* ADA, *at her pale, anguished face grimacing with pain.* NESSIE *reaches out to stroke her black hair.*

NESSIE: Ohh so soft. Soft.

AUNT MORAG: One of God's difficult daughters. Yet, one can feel *him* in her, frightening like a storm.

129. EXT. BAINES'S HUT. DUSK.

BAINES *rides up to his house in the evening light. He is silly with happiness.* HIRA *comes running out to meet him.*

HIRA: *Peini, Peini,* liddle gel. I seen her come up here, scream, scream, scream . . . Blood on her. Look bad . . . Very bad . . .

BAINES *jumps off his horse and strides into his hut.*

130. INT. BAINES'S HUT. DUSK.

Inside he finds FLORA *crouching in a corner; her face is white, tear-stained and splattered with mud. Her angel wings are squashed behind her and blood-stained. On seeing* BAINES *she cries with renewed pain and relief.*

BAINES: What has happened? Hush, hush, what is it?

FLORA *thrusts the wrapped finger at* BAINES. *He takes the blood-soaked object and unwraps it. The finger unravels into his hand; he reels back groaning, choking, about to be sick.*

FLORA (*Yelling.*): He says you're not to see her or he'll chop her up!

BAINES (*Angry, horrified.*): What happened?

But FLORA *cannot speak. She bursts into loud sobs.*

BAINES *kneels in front of her, shaking her.*

TELL ME! TELL ME!

BAINES *stops shaking her; she scrambles away and out of the door.*

BAINES *chases after her.*

131. EXT. BAINES'S HUT. DUSK.

FLORA *screams as he catches her.*

BAINES: Quiet down! Shhh! Where is she?

FLORA (*Whimpering.*): He chopped it off! He chopped it off!

BAINES: Jesus! I'll kill him! I'll kill him!

FLORA: No, no. Don't go near!

BAINES: What did she say to him? (*Shaking her.*) What?

HIRA: Put her down, *Peini.* She jus' liddle.

HIRA *takes the quivering* FLORA *in her arms.*

There, girl, there . . .

BAINES *notices the blood on* FLORA's *dress; he touches it, she shies away.*

132. EXT. STEWART'S HUT. NIGHT.

STEWART *walks outside his hut, disconsolate.*

133. INT. STEWART'S HUT. NIGHT.

STEWART *enters* ADA's *room with a lamp. He puts it down beside her on the table. He studies her pale face and dry lips.* ADA's *eyes flicker open.*

STEWART (*Speaking to his feet.*): I lost my temper. I'm sorry.

STEWART *looks at* ADA.

STEWART: You broke my trust, you pushed me hard, too hard. (*He sighs.*) You cannot send love to HIM, you cannot do it . . . Even to think on it makes me angry, very angry . . .

ADA *opens her eyes and looks at* STEWART. *It is evident she hears nothing and has understood nothing, she is*

111

struggling with pain. Her face grimaces and she groans.

STEWART: I meant to love you. I clipped your wing, that is all.

STEWART *sings two lines of an English love ballad to* ADA.

STEWART: We shall be together, you will see it will be better . . .

Her forehead is damp with fever. She thrashes at the blankets. STEWART *pulls them off to cool her. He feels her brow.*

STEWART: (*Whispering.*): . . . My love bird.

Her nightgown is damp with sweat and clings to her body. STEWART *reaches out to adjust her gown; his hand touches her leg and he holds it there, feeling a tingle of pleasure that grows and builds the longer his hand remains.*

STEWART: Ohhhhh my love . . .

His hand begins to move further and further up her leg, nudging the nightgown higher and higher. He looks at her face. She is closed-eyed, unconscious. STEWART's *face crinkles into a pained expression and all his control melts into a drive to hold and extend this moment. He brings his mouth to her leg and begins to kiss her knee, her thigh. A new thought occurs to him, a terrible thought, but as he has phrased the thought to himself, he cannot resist it. He glances at her face, still fevered and unconscious. Quietly, stealthily, he begins to undo his belt buckle. He bends across her to gently separate her legs. As he moves his body over her, he looks towards her, and to his shame and horror she is looking directly back at him, her eyes perfectly on his, perfectly focused. Quietly* STEWART *moves back and pulls down her gown, all the time keeping his eyes on her.*

STEWART: You are feeling better?

ADA's *lips move slightly and* STEWART *turns suddenly as if he has heard something. Slowly he turns back to* ADA.

STEWART *looks at* ADA *intently, moving closer to her bed, closer to* ADA, *his eyes locked on hers.*

STEWART: What . . .?

The sound of his own voice makes him blink. He watches her as if listening to her speak in a voice that is so faint, and distant that only with great concentration and perseverance can he make it out. As he watches her his face transforms; his eyes fill, his lips soften and his eyebrows take on the exact expression of her own.

The kerosene lamp burns fitfully, fluttering a light pulse across their faces. STEWART *moves closer to* ADA. *Outside a wind bangs the iron roof and rubs branches against each other, making a high-pitched see-saw sound. He leans closer still.*

134. EXT. STEWART'S HUT. NIGHT.

STEWART *carrying a candle in a glass box makes his way through ghostly tree stumps. In his other arm he has his gun.*

135. EXT./INT. BAINES'S HUT. NIGHT.

At BAINES's *hut* STEWART *steps over the curled figure of* HIRA *sleeping on the verandah and walks through the hut towards the bedroom where a lit candle flickers.*

136. INT. BAINES'S BEDROOM. NIGHT.

In the bed lies FLORA *wrapped in a blanket with* BAINES *beside her, axe in hand, both fast asleep.* STEWART *nudges* BAINES *awake with the butt of his rifle, prodding him under the chin.* BAINES *wakes rudely with a start, frozen by the sight of* STEWART *with his rifle.*

STEWART: Put that away, on the floor.

BAINES *obeys, careful not to disturb the sleeping child.*
STEWART *sits near the bed on a box, resting his gun
across his knee; his face is glowing; he looks closely at*
BAINES, *examining him.*

STEWART: I look at you, at your face. I have had that face
    in my head, hating it. But now I am here seeing it . . .
    It's nothing, you blink, you have your mark, you look
    at me through your eyes, yes, you are even scared of
    me . . .

STEWART *laughs.*

STEWART: Look at you!

BAINES *watches him stiffly, disconcerted, unable to read*
STEWART*'s strange mood.* STEWART *stares back at him.*

STEWART (*Softly.*): Has Ada ever spoken to you?

BAINES: You mean in signs?

STEWART: No, words. You have never heard words?

BAINES: No, not words.

STEWART *nods.*

STEWART: Never thought you heard words?

BAINES *shakes his head.*

STEWART (*Slowly.*): She has spoken to me. I heard her
    voice. There was no sound, but I heard it here. (*He
    presses his forehead with the palm of his hand.*) Her
    voice was there in my head. I watched her lips, they
    did not make the words, yet the harder I listened the
    clearer I heard her, as clear as I hear you, as clear as I
    hear my own voice.

BAINES (*Trying to understand.*): Spoken words?

STEWART: No, but her words are in my head. (*He looks at*
    BAINES *and pauses.*) I know what you think, that it's a
    trick, that I'm making it up. No, the words I heard
    were her words.

BAINES (*Suspiciously.*): What are they?

STEWART *looks up at the ceiling as if reciting something he has learnt by heart and means to repeat exactly as he heard it:*

STEWART: She said, 'I have to go, let me go, let Baines take me away, let him try and save me. I am frightened of my will, of what it might do, it is so strange and strong.'

BAINES, *recovering himself, eyes* STEWART *angrily.*

BAINES: You punished her wrongly, it was me, my fault.

STEWART *does not answer. Finally he looks up, his eyes full with tears.*

STEWART: Understand me, I am here for her, for her . . . I wonder that I don't wake, that I am not asleep to be here talking with you. I love her. But what is the use? She doesn't care for me. I wish her gone. I wish you gone. I want to wake and find it was a dream, that is what I want. I want to believe I am not this man. I want myself back; the one I knew.

FLORA *moves and turns in her sleep. The two men watch. Her brow frowns, then smooths. Her eyelids roll as her eyes dart back and forth in dream.*

137. EXT. STREAM NEAR BAINES'S HUT. DAY.
HIRA *washes out the mud from* FLORA'*s dress and angel wings in a bush stream.*

138. INT./EXT. STEWART'S HUT. DAY.
ADA'*s trunks are delivered outside* STEWART'*s hut by* AUNT MORAG *and her girls.* ADA *is led from* STEWART'*s hut by* NESSIE. *She wears a black dress and her arm is tied in a white sling. The light outside makes her blink.* NESSIE *smooths her hair behind her shoulders.* FLORA *timidly peeps at her mother from behind* BAINES.

139. EXT. BUSH ON WAY TO BEACH. DAY.
The piano is carried on ahead, while in the secrecy of the bush BAINES *kisses* ADA *passionately. She looks back at him, worried.*

140. EXT. STEWART'S HUT. DAY.
STEWART *lays out ten guns in front of his hut door. The* MAORI NEGOTIATIOR *and his people inspect them. The* MAORI NEGOTIATOR *signals he wants the blankets too.*

141. EXT. BEACH. DAY.
On the beach ADA *sits looking out to sea while* FLORA *plaits her hair in one thick braid behind her back. She places the bonnet carefully on top. At the sea edge in front of them the piano is being loaded on the canoe.*

142. EXT. BEACH. DAY.
HIRA *and* BAINES *are next to each other by the canoe.* HIRA *is looking at* ADA.
HIRA: I worry for you.
BAINES: No, I love her, we will be a family. I have her piano. I will mend it, she will get better. I worry for you.
HIRA (*Grumpily*): Oh, I'm ooright . . . got my tobacco. In the end, can we lose? No, we turn the *pakeha* gun on the *pakeha* and get our land back. Pow! Pow!

143. EXT. AT SEA/BEACH. DAY.
The sea is choppy and the piano is difficult to steady in the canoe. BAINES *helps with the rigging of the piano; thick rope ends coil under the women's feet.*
MAORI OARSMAN: *Tarmaharawa – aianei tahuri ai.*
    [*Subtitled*: It's too heavy – the canoe will tip over.]

BAINES: *Keite pai! Kaare e titahataha ana.*

   [*Subtitled*: It's all right! Look, it's nicely balanced.]
HIRA: Leave it, *Peini* – it too heavy.
BAINES: No, she needs it, she must have it!
ANOTHER OARSMAN (*Shrugging.*): *Te hau – Kua. Kaha ke
   te pupuhi.*

   [*Subtitled*: The wind is already strong.]

144. EXT. BEACH. DAY.
HIRA *is left on the shore with one child and two other*
MAORI PEOPLE. *Tears run openly down her big sad face as
she sings her farewell to* BAINES.
HIRA: *He rimu teretere koe ete. Peini eeeii,*
       Tere Ki Tawhiti Ki Pamamao eeeii
       He waka Teretere He waka teretere.
       Ko koe ka tere ki tua whakarere eeeii.
       [You are like seaweed drifting in the sea, Baines,
       Drift far away, drift far beyond the horizon.
       A canoe glides hither, a canoe glides thither,
       But you though will journey on and eventually
       be beyond the veil.*

145. EXT. AT/BEACH. DAY.
The canoe has paddled away from the shore. FLORA *leans
over the edge of the canoe, her mouth, her hair held back
by* BAINES.
FLORA: I can't . . .
BAINES *rubs her back.* FLORA *straightens up.*

   I can't.
They retake their seats, FLORA's *back to the piano, while*
BAINES *sits next to* ADA. *He tenderly takes her good hand.*

* Verse by courtesy of Selwyn Muru.

117

ADA *removes hers and signs to* FLORA, *who looks at her mother, then* BAINES *amazed.*

BAINES: What did she say?

FLORA (*Puzzled.*): She says, throw the piano overboard.

BAINES (*To* ADA): It's quite safe, they are managing . . .

ADA *signs again.*

BAINES (*Anxiously*): What?

FLORA: She says, throw it overboard. She doesn't want it.
     She says it's spoiled.

BAINES: I have the key here, look, I'll have it mended . . .

ADA (*Mimes directly to* BAINES): 'PUSH IT OVER'. (*Her
     determination is increasing.*)

MAORI OARSMAN: *Ae! Peia. Turakina! Bushit! Peia te
     kawheha kite moana.*
     [*Subtitled*: Yeah, she's right, push it over, push the
     coffin in the water.]

BAINES (*Softly, urgently*): Please, Ada, you will regret it.
     It's your piano, I want you to have it.

But ADA *does not listen, she is adamant and begins to
untie the ropes.*

FLORA (*Panicking.*): She doesn't want IT!

The canoe is unbalancing as ADA *struggles with the ropes.*

BAINES: All right, sit down, sit down.

ADA *sits, pleased. Her eyes glow and her face is now alive.*

     BAINES *speaks to the* MAORIS, *who stop paddling, and
together they loosen the ropes securing the piano to the
canoe.*

     As they manoeuvre the piano to the edge ADA *looks
into the water. She puts her hand into the sea and moves it
back and forth.*

     *The piano is carefully lowered and with a heave topples
over. As the piano splashes into the sea, the loose ropes
speed their way after it.* ADA *watches them snake past her*

120

feet and then, out of a fatal curiosity, odd and
undisciplined, she steps into a loop.
    The rope tightens and grips her foot so that she is
snatched into the sea, and pulled by the piano down
through the cold water.

146. INT. SEA NEAR BEACH. DAY.
Bubbles tumble from her mouth. Down she falls, on and
on, her eyes are open, her clothes twisting about her. The
MAORIS *diving after her cannot reach her in these depths.*
ADA *begins to struggle. She kicks at the rope, but it holds*
tight around her boot. She kicks hard again and then, with
her other foot, levers herself free from her shoe. The piano
and her shoe continue their fall while ADA *floats above,*
suspended in deep water, then suddenly her body awakes
and fights, struggling upwards to the surface.

147. AT SEA BEACH. DAY.
As ADA *breaks the surface her VOICE OVER begins:*
ADA (V.O.):
        What a death!
        What a chance!
        What a surprise!
        My will has chosen life!?
        Still it has had me spooked, and many others
        besides!
ADA, *coughing and spluttering, is pulled on to the canoe.*
She is wrapped in jackets and blankets.

148. INT. SEA NEAR BEACH. DAY.
Underwater we see the canoe bottom, its oars dipping the
surface.

149. INT. ADA'S NELSON DRAWING ROOM. DUSK.
ADA (V.O.):

> I teach piano now in Nelson. George has
> fashioned me a metal fingertip; I am quite the
> town freak, which satisfies.
>
> I am learning to speak. My sound is still so
> bad I feel ashamed. I practise only when I am
> alone and it is dark.

ADA's *hands move across the piano keys; her metal finger shines in the dull light.*

DISSOLVE TO:

150. INT. ADA'S NELSON DRAWING ROOM. NIGHT.
ADA *paces up and down the small drawing room. There are no lights on, only a dim blue evening wash. Over her head she has a dark cloth; her voice makes low, guttural sounds as it repeats the vowels.*

DISSOLVE TO:

151. INT. SEA BED NEAR BEACH. DAY.
ADA (V.O.):

> At night I think of my piano in its ocean grave,
> and sometimes of myself floating above it.
> Down there everything is so still and silent that
> it lulls me to sleep. It is a weird lullaby and so
> it is; it is mine.

ADA's *piano on the sea bed, its lid fallen away. Above floats* ADA, *her hair and arms stretched out in a gesture of surrender, her body slowly turning on the end of the rope. The seaweed's rust-coloured fronds reach out to touch her.*

ADA (V.O.):
    THERE IS A SILENCE WHERE HATH BEEN NO SOUND
    THERE IS A SILENCE WHERE NO SOUND MAY BE
    IN THE COLD GRAVE, UNDER THE DEEP DEEP SEA.*

* Thomas Hood (1799–1845): 'Sonnet: Silence'.

NOTES AND EXTRA DIALOGUE

1   Scene 10. SEAMEN'S DISCUSSION.
    The wind and the low manner of their speaking
    makes it impossible to hear the exact nature of
    the discussion.
    – 'Tis a dead shore, a dead shore.
    – Leave her alone, it's what she wanted.
    – A pox on you!
    – Ay, very nice, leave her and be lynched for the
      pleasure.
    – Do what you like, I'm off this shore.
      etc.

2   Scene 12. ART DEPARTMENT NOTE.
    ADA's finger is seen *inside* the dark crate,
    sounding a few notes.

3   Scene 15. TRANSLATION NOTE.
    (i) with the Maori language dialogue of BAINES
    and the MAORI PEOPLE, the general scheme is
    that only when necessary to sense or humour will
    subtitled translation be given. However, for the
    benefit of its readers, this script will translate
    everything; what will be subtitled is noted. See
    also the Glossary, p. 131.

    (ii) Extra Maori dialogue, Scene 15.
        – *Awe!*
          [What was that?]
        – *He Kehua?*
          [Is it a ghost?]
        PARA *and* TU *are making bird calls.*

E kii ha manu kourua!
E tiko manu ana kourua?
[So you think you're birds!
Do you actually shit like birds?]

(iii) Many of the MAORIS have coughs, running
noses and sores. (They have no immunity to
European diseases.)

(iv) Maori names.
MEN

Tu	*Tame*
Pito	*Hotu*
Hone	*Para*
Tipi	*Kaha* (boy)

WOMEN

Tai	*Ani*

4   Scene 19.
(i) Background dialogue for beginning of scene
   – *He ahu te raruraru*
     [*Subtitled*: What happened?]
   – *I konei tonu, ka moe te koroua nei.*
     [*Subtitled*: He just decided to go to sleep]

(ii) Background dialogue for end of scene
   – *Taiho. Kei muri pea inga rakau nei. Aue!*
     Tino matatoru konei.
     Me haere ake ano an ki runga.
     [Hold on, maybe behind this clump. Gee,
     the undergrowth is thick here. I'll come up
     again.]
   – *Kahore ne huarahi – kahorene tutae.*
     [No track, no shit]

5   Scene 29. ADA's piano piece, duration approximately 90 seconds.

6   Scene 30. Duet, 20–30 seconds.

7   Scene 33. FLORA's singing, 20 seconds.

8   Scene 34. HENI/MARY phrasing of National Anthem:

HENI/MARY

        Got safe ah gayshy Quin
        Long lif a gayshy Quin
        Got shayf a Quin
        Shendah Wikitoria
        Har - py en a Clohria
        Long to rain ourush
        Got Safe ah Quin

9   Scene 37. Translation note:

        Who is that rumbles within?
        Is it Ruaumoko, is it Ruaumoko?
        Jab, smash, jab, smash
        Jab, smash, jab, smash
        The Taniwha, the Taniwha.
        That is within . . . He!

10   Scene 65. The mud around the school hall is so deep that a labyrinth of planks is set up to avoid it.

11   Scene 87. Extra dialogue.

MAORI PIANO BEARERS

    – *Tahi Patene ruapuri patene*
      Tekau patene ornatekau pwari patene
      [One button, two bloody buttons.
      Ten buttons, twenty bloody buttons.]

    – *Kia Whai tarau ano ra monga patene!*
      [We needs pants for the buttons eh!]
    – *He patene te kai, he patene te kai*
      A popo ka tiko patene ahau patene
      ma nga tangata katoa.
      [Buttons for food, buttons for food.
      Buttons for everybody. By tomorrow I'll be
      shitting buttons.]

12   Scene 100. Approximately 60 seconds of ADA's
      piano playing.

GLOSSARY

haka	Maori war dance
kuia	elderly or senior womenfolk
kumera	sweet potato
mana	honour, prestige
Moko	facial tatoo
Pa	Maori village based around a meeting house
pakeha	white person
Peini	Baines's Maori name
pipi	small shellfish
Tapu	sacred, forbidden
toi-toi	large New Zealand plant with feathery plumes
Tupeka	tobacco

CAST LIST

Ada	Holly Hunter
Baines	Harvey Keitel
Stewart	Sam Neill
Flora	Anna Paquin
Aunt Morag	Kerry Walker
Nessie	Geneviève Lemon
Hira	Tungia Baker
Reverend	Ian Mune
Head seaman	Peter Dennett
Chief Nihe	Te Whatanui Skipwith
Hone	Pete Smith
Blind piano tuner	Bruce Allpress
Mana	Cliff Curtis
Heni (Mission girl)	Carla Rupuha
Mary (Mission girl)	Mahina Tunui
Muturu	Hori Ahipene
Te Kori	Gordon Hatfield
Chief Nihe's daughter	Mere Boynton
Marama	Kirsten Batley
Mahina	Tania Burney
Te Tiwha	Annie Edwards
Roimata	Harina Haare
Parearau	Christina Harimate
Amohia	Steve Kanuta
Taua	P. J. Karauria
Tame	Sonny Kirikiri
Kahutia	Alain Makiha
Tipi	Greg Mayor
Tahu	Neil Mika Gudsell
Kohuru	Guy Moana

Rehia	Joseph Otimi
Mairangi	Glynis Paraha
Rongo	Riki Pickering
Pitama	Eru Potaka-Dewes
Te Ao	Liane Rangi Henry
Te Hikumutu	Huihana Rewa
Pito	Tamati Rice
Hotu	Paora Sharples
Tuu	George Smallman
Tu Kukuni	Kereama Teua

CREW

Director	Jane Campion
Writer	Jane Campion
Producer	Jan Chapman
Executive producer	Alain Depardieu
Associate producer	Mark Turnbull
Director of photography	Stuart Dryburgh
Production designer	Andrew McAlpine
Costume designer	Janet Patterson
Music composed by	Michael Nyman
Editor	Veronika Jenet

Casting Directors:

New Zealand	Diana Rowan
United Kingdom	Susie Figgis
United States	Victoria Thomas
Maori dialogue and advisers	Waihoroi Shortland
	Selwyn Muru
Sound designer	Lee Smith
Production manager	Chloe Smith
1st assistant director	Mark Turnbull
Stills	Grant Matthews
	Polly Walker

THE MAKING OF *THE PIANO*

Jane Campion began writing *The Piano* in 1984, even before the making of her first feature film *Sweetie* (1989) and long before her direction of *An Angel at My Table* (1990).

Although she was living and working in Sydney, her imagination was drawn back to the colonial past of her birth country, New Zealand:

CAMPION: I think that it's a strange heritage that I have as a *pakeha* New Zealander, and I wanted to be in a position to touch or explore that. In contrast to the original people in New Zealand, the Maori people, who have such an attachment to history, we seem to have no history, or at least not the same tradition. This makes you start to ask, 'Well, who are my ancestors?' My ancestors are English colonizers – the people who came out like Ada and Stewart and Baines.

Having invented these three fictional nineteenth-century forebears, Campion set them into a highly charged love triangle in order to explore the way erotic impulses and the unpredictable emotions that can arise through their enactment might have been experienced in another century, another landscape:

CAMPION: I have enjoyed writing characters who don't have a twentieth-century sensibility about sex. They have nothing to prepare themselves for its strength and power. We grew up with all those magazines that described courtship, giving us lots of little rules and

ways of handling it. We grow up with so many expectations around it, that it's almost like the pure sexual erotic impulse is lost to us. But for them . . . the husband Stewart had probably never had sex at all. So for him to experience sex or feelings of sexual jealousy would have been personality-transforming. The impact of sex is not softened, it's cleaner and extremer for that.

Some three years after its inception, Jane Campion showed the first draft of the script of *The Piano* to Jan Chapman, who would produce the film. Chapman and Campion had worked at the ABC together when Chapman invited Campion to direct the telefeature *Two Friends* in 1986. Chapman was compelled by what she read:

CHAPMAN: I felt terribly excited by it. It reminded me of things in my adolescence that were very strong, ideas that I had formed from reading romantic literature, that feeling that passion is all, that living for your desires is a way of taking on life to its fullest.

Juggling other film projects, the two began to meet with Billy McKinnon for a series of script development sessions:

CAMPION: One of the major changes to the script was to give the ending a more poetical, more psychological finish.
CHAPMAN: It really needed the right ending or it could have been too soft. But basically Jane – with our help – came up with the idea of the erotic focus shifting for Ada, from the lover Baines to her husband Stewart. I think this is the thing that makes the film modern actually, and not sentimental.
CAMPION: Ada actually uses her husband Stewart as a sexual object – this is the outrageous morality of the film – which seems very innocent but in fact has its power to be very surprising. I think many women have had the

experience of feeling like a sexual object, and that's exactly what happens to Stewart. The cliché of that situation is generally the other way around, where men say things like, 'Oh, sex for its own sake.' But to see a woman actually doing it, especially a Victorian woman, is somehow shocking – and to see a man so vulnerable. It becomes a relationship of power, the power of those that care and those that don't care. I'm very very interested in the brutal innocence of that.

Campion set the script against a backdrop of parallel intensity and intimacy, the New Zealand bush:

CAMPION: The bush has got an enchanted, complex, even frightening quality to it, unlike anything that you see anywhere else. It's mossy and very intimate, and there's an underwater look that's always charmed me. I was after the vivid, subconscious imagery of the bush, its dark, inner world.

The instinctive game that I felt we needed to play was that, while the epic style of the film and landscape suggest the romantic genre, at the same time the people seem very real – so that you're never quite let out by any sense that the action is taking place in a fairy tale or romantic world. One of the clichés of romance is that the heroines are classic beauties, but I wanted there to be a reality to our actors that counters pure romanticism.

We're all dealing with fiction here, but the sensation of authenticity around the look is really important. That sensation can be created in a lot of ways – one of which was to give our heroine greasy hair. If you look at early photographs they always have really greasy hair. Most people when they do period movies certainly don't include that. But whereas many actresses would feel it was going to make them look hard, Holly was game and went along with it. I think it is things like this that give the film and the character a really different look: hairdos which are strange but also authentic. And they are hard, but then the lighting is predisposed to empathy with the character; we keep playing these different messages.

I feel a kinship between the kind of romance that Emily Brontë portrayed in *Wuthering Heights* and this film. Hers is not the notion of romance that we've come to use, it's very harsh and extreme, a gothic exploration of the romantic impulse. I wanted to respond to those ideas in my own century.

My not writing in Emily's time means that I can look at a side of relationship that it wasn't possible to do then. My exploration can be a lot more sexual, a lot more investigative of the power of eroticism, which can add another dimension. Because then you get involved in the actual bodyscape of it as well, because the body has certain effects, like a drug almost, certain desires for erotic satisfaction which are very strong forces too.

Andrew McAlpine, the production designer, remembers that, in addition to the complicated and numerous set constructions, they also altered every landscape in some way to enhance or heighten the feeling or mood of a particular scene:

McALPINE: Take the burning stump and mud landscape surrounding Stewart's house. Here we transplanted and charred dead trees to create the illusion of a very muddy five acres of primary slash and burn. I wanted the bride to be seen to be drawn into this dank darkness that is Stewart's and then to step out into this green cathedral of *nikau* and *punga* that is Baines's life: a very gothic landscape, surrounded by this cool green light.

Also, the setting for the scene where Stewart attacks Ada on the path to Baines's hut. This had too much openness, so we gave it a web of supplejack. It's such an incredible feature of New Zealand bush, this anarchical, black-branched creeper. It's very tough: you can't break it. So we devised this huge net, this horrible tentacled nightmare inside which Ada and Stewart struggle.

The director of photography was Stuart Dryburgh, for whom the main attraction of the story was the perversity of it all:

DRYBURGH: We're dealing with a costume drama, which implies many things, and yet Jane's approach has been totally irreverent. The period is a setting that allows certain extremes to occur, but I found it to be a very contemporary story.

The camera's viewpoint on all this is that of a witness directing the viewer's attention in a very intimate way. Sometimes we go places where the camera can't really go. We've been inside the piano, inside Stewart's pocket, right down at the level of hands and fingers and tea cups. It wouldn't be a Jane Campion film without some wittiness in the framing.

For the cinematography, we've used a nineteenth-century colour stills process process – the autochrome – as an inspiration. That's why we've tended to use strong colour accents in different parts of the film, drawing out the blue-greens of the bush and the amber-rich mud. Part of the director's brief was that we would echo the film's element of underwater in the bush. 'Bottom of the fish tank' was the description we used for ourselves to help define what we were looking for. So we played it murky blue-green and let the skin tones sit down in amongst it.

We tried not to light the bush ourselves but to work only with the natural light wherever possible. It's a strange light, a light that comes from above, but also from many different directions at once. There can be very sudden gradients of light and shade from a blaze of sunlight coming through the canopy to the darkest shadow in a creek bed, and these will happen within inches of each other. We've tried to represent it honestly, and let it be a dark place.

Sally Sherratt, the location finder, took some four weeks to cast the beaches of black sand and cliff, topped by bush of almost prehistoric density – and mud. In fact this landscape was to be a hybrid creation of distant and neighbouring locations jigsawed together to represent the lush difference of old New Zealand. She recalls how 'Jane said very clearly what she wanted. Each location was to have its particular feeling and meaning – and she warned me, "Beware of the Bland Old Bush!" '

Jan Chapman remembers the first meeting between Campion and Sherratt:

CHAPMAN: It was unlike any kind of location meeting I've ever witnessed, because it was so detailed. You think bush is bush but Sally and Jane were having this conversation that was really quite lyrical and passionate – about different kinds of trees! Being an Australian I didn't really know the New Zealand bush. I have a feeling for it now – it was really a major player in the film. And now I also feel that it is very much part of New Zealand, that the relationship to the land is fundamental there.

Essential to the truth of the period was the inclusion of a Maori 'story'. Campion felt keenly aware of their place in the film, and of the need for Maori advisers and writers to help create such a story:

CAMPION: Even though it's a European story, which is what I am – European – I determined that it would involve having Maori people in the film. Cross-cultural collaborations are sensitive, and for me it was a pretty scary endeavour. It wasn't without tears and difficulty. But I think people were actually pleased to have a position where there could be a meeting. You just don't get opportunities to experience that in everyday kiwi society. In the end the cross-cultural quality of it was one of the deeply moving aspects of being on the production for us all, cast and crew.

The result of the collaboration is a large Maori cast, who lend an extraordinarily rich collective presence to the film. An aspect of this visibility is the display of traditional Maori body culture. Gordon Hatfield, himself a carver, who displays on screen an authentic buttock tattoo in a traditional design of his tribe (the 'Nga Puki'), explains: 'In our culture, the whole body is considered a temple.' Most striking are facial tattoos (*moko*) that symbolized the wearer's status and spiritual power (*mana*) within tribal Maori society.

For Harvey Keitel, as George Baines, the Maori presence was equally important:

KEITEL: Baines has given up his culture – he's not a *pakeha* and he's not a Maori. He's nowhere, looking for a place to be, and he finds it through his ability to suffer, through his ability to go on a journey to find what he needs. He's interested in the possibility of having a union, a family, a relationship.

In common with Baines, Keitel was struck by the way in which the Maori cast, in role and out of role 'tend to have a more profound relationship to the earth and the spirits than the *pakeha* do':

KEITEL: I was very affected by Tungia, the woman playing Hira in the film. She came down to Karekare beach, and

the first thing she did was cross the beach to the sea, bend over and sprinkle herself with water. And I said 'What are you doing?' And she said, 'I'm asking the sea to welcome me.'

In 1990, Chapman and Campion set out on a long fund-raising tour. In the end the solution was provided by financial investment from one source, the French company CIBY 2000.

CHAPMAN: CIBY was a new company that we believed in because they appeared to have a commitment to the creative freedom of the film-maker. They had previously funded films by David Lynch, Pedro Almodóvar and were scheduling a production with Bertolucci. We decided to take a mutual, creative risk with each other. The representative of CIBY, Alain Depardieu, allowed us to make the story our way, while being present to provide a strong communication link with the French company.

For what was to be 'a French-financed, New Zealand-based, Australian production of a New Zealand story', Chapman and Campion were keen to cast internationally. Campion, who had established a reputation for drawing strong performances from less experienced actors, was seeking another kind of challenge:

CAMPION: I wanted to work with actors who would throw me into a different arena, to be called forth myself by actors who were demanding and experienced. The characters in the script needed to be 'owned' by actors who could take them on, control them, and have the experience to do so.

In fact the script itself was a large factor in drawing that experience. Campion had long had her fellow countryman Sam Neill in mind for the part of Stewart:

NEILL: I remember meeting Jane at the Berlin Film Festival and saying, 'Of course I think of Stewart as being an archetypal *pakeha* New Zealand male, greedy for land and so on.' And Jane was very surprised; she by no means saw Stewart as the villain of the piece – which I found extremely encouraging. Certainly he serves that function from time to time, but he is not the villain. I don't condone what he does, but I see it as entirely understandable because of the time he lives in: and he's a man of his time.

I think this film explores both the desperate and the wonderful things that happen between men and women in a way that's not often done in films. And these things make for moments of sublime ecstasy and moments of the most terrible fear, of terror. It's been pretty scary territory to be acting in – it helps to have had a little life experience.

I see Stewart as being someone who is rather vulnerable. There are certain sad things about him: lonelinesses. What happens to him, I think, is that this shell – a carapace that Victorian men could assume – is cracked and disintegrated by the power of his feelings for Ada, leaving him very exposed. I think of him as being a man who has lost all his skin.

For the film's potent heart, Ada, Chapman recalls:

CHAPMAN: There was a long list of extraordinary possibilities, from Australian actresses to a number of French, English or Americans. We could have been unimaginative enough to have not seen Holly Hunter because the Holly of *Broadcast News* and our Ada were

two entirely different people. Ada was going to be a tall woman with a strong, dark, eerie, Frida Kahlo sort of beauty. But in Holly's audition tape her gaze was just stupendous.

For Hunter, the script had 'one ingredient that almost every script I read does not have: a vast dimension of things being unexplained to the audience or even to the characters themselves – and that's just a real haunting part of the story, very, very haunting . . .'

HUNTER: The costumes helped me tremendously: the incongruity of having a woman in a really laced-up corset, huge hoop skirts, petticoats, pantaloons, bodice and chemise trying to gracefully manoeuvre her way through the bush, was a real physical manifestation of Ada. That's what women of that period dealt with, that's how they developed: there was an obvious physical fragility – and yet strength and stamina, as well as grace, were required to wear those clothes. That was an interesting dichotomy that the period offered me.

I think Jane was very brave in holding out for a more original kind of sexuality and sensuous quality in Ada. Jane really was interested in redefining for herself what you could come to call beautiful in Ada as the story unfolds: from the hairdos, to the severity of the costumes. I'm amazed that she was able to capture this nineteenth-century woman without conventional morals. Ada had her own personal set of morals that guided her; society's did not really touch her. She didn't really have shame or guilt in her make-up.

Hunter also brought to the role of Ada a talent unhoped for: the piano skills that were to be crucial in the definition of her silent, screen character's 'voice'.

The composer, Michael Nyman, met Hunter in New York in the pre-production period:

NYMAN: I needed to ascertain purely physical things like whether she was capable of playing fast or slow, how big her stretch was and so on. I had noticed from the tape she sent me that she was much more adept at powerful, emotional pieces than very precise, rhythmic things. I had to find music which she, Holly, the pianist and the actress, rather than her character, was emotionally attracted to, so that she could really be engaged by it and give it passion.

I had to establish not only a repertoire of music for the film, but a repertoire of piano music that would have been Ada's repertoire as a pianist, almost as if she had been the composer of it.

Since Ada was from Scotland, it was logical to use Scottish folk and popular songs as the basis for our music. Once I hit on that idea the whole thing fell into place. It's as though I've been writing the music of another composer who happened to live in Scotland, then New Zealand in the mid 1850s. Someone who was obviously not a professional composer or pianist, so there had to be a modesty to it.

Music is absolutely crucial to the film. Since Ada doesn't speak, the piano music doesn't simply have the usual expressive role but becomes a substitute for her voice. The sound of the piano becomes her character, her mood, her expressions, her unspoken dialogue. It has to convey the messages she is putting across about her feelings towards Baines during the piano lessons. I've had to create a kind of aural scenography which is as important as the locations, as important as the costumes.

The film score also has to be written in such a way that it's my music, recognizably me. Ideally you keep your identity, and allow the project to stretch you.

Hunter, who'd learnt piano into late adolescence, had only recently started playing again when she was cast as Ada: 'It was a formidable, frightening task. I didn't know if I was going to be able to play in front of people. But I had to play so often and so much that in the end I could.'

In mid-1991 Campion and Chapman flew to LA to cast another surprise – Harvey Keitel. Of their work together Campion comments:

CAMPION: The nice thing about Harvey is that he's not a young actor and he's not an old actor, he's ageless in a way. His commitment to acting and his philosophy about it is absolutely staunch and excited. For me, he brought a whole alertness and awareness of the acting tradition, he's one of those people that really live it.

Campion charged the New Zealand casting agent Di Rowan with finding *The Piano*'s fourth protagonist, Flora. After a country-wide search and a stack of audition tapes, Campion finally set eyes on her – a young girl called Anna Paquin:

CAMPION: I remember when I first saw the audition tape. Anna came on and there was this tiny little girl, probably the smallest of all I'd seen – and extremely shy. I almost turned it off. I thought this girl was never going to be able to cope with this huge speech. I just about fell off my chair when she began. She just looked into the camera and never blinked. She told this long, extremely impassioned story of how Ada lost her voice, and you totally believed her. It's a remarkable experience to see someone so young with such an instinct for performance.

The relationship of Flora to her mother was scripted by Campion to be one of mirror-like closeness, a kind of symbiosis. As Andrew McAlpine comments: 'The complicity between Ada and Flora is frightening, like a Diane Arbus photograph. Beautiful, too, because it's so tender – and Holly and Anna turned out to be extraordinary people together.' Campion was particularly delighted at the parallel complicity that grew between the American actor and the girl, whose 'glorious instincts' Hunter praised. According to Campion, 'Anna never really crashed as we were told that children do in movies over long periods of time. I think the great thing was that she had Holly – and they adored each other from the first. They were an incredible team – Anna would use all Holly's mannerisms of performance.'

Faced with a script that gives her a mysteriously silent mother Anna comments:

ANNA: Some of the time I think Ada's a bit weird. Like, what happened to her that she doesn't speak? She hasn't spoken since she was 6 years old!

I even liked Holly the first day I met her – because of the way she was told by Jane not to talk on set, so I could get used to having a mother who does not talk.

Asked whether she felt there was a likeness between her and Flora, she claims there is only 'a wee bit. Actually, she tells more lies than I do.'

For Campion, the commitment of actors like those in this film was 'awesome': 'They bring with them a particular responsibility for their character, and woe betide you if you were to do anything to hurt their character or diminish them.'

MIRO BILBROUGH (from the Production Notes)

JANE CAMPION

Jane Campion was born in Wellington, New Zealand, and now lives in Sydney, Australia. Having graduated with a BA in Anthropology from Victoria University of Wellington in 1975, and a BA, with Painting Major, at Sydney College of Arts in 1979, she began film-making in the early 1980s, attending the Australian School of Film and Television. Her first short film, *Peel* (1982), won the Palme D'Or at the Cannes Film Festival in 1986. Her other short films are *Passionless Moments* (1984), *A Girl's Own Story* (1983), *After Hours* (1984) and the telefeature *Two Friends* (1986), all of which won Australian and international awards.

Campion co-wrote and directed her first feature film, *Sweetie* (1989), which won the Georges Sadoul Prize in 1989 for Best Foreign Film, as well as the LA Film Critics' New Generation Award in 1990, the American Independent Spirit Award for Best Foreign Feature and the Australian Critics' Award for Best Film, Best Director and Best Actress. She followed this with *An Angel at My Table* (1990), a dramatization based on the autobiographies of Janet Frame which won some seven prizes, including the Silver Lion at the Venice Film Festival in 1990. It was also awarded prizes at Toronto and Berlin, again winning the American Independent Spirit Award, and was voted the most popular film at the 1990 Sydney Film Festival. Her latest feature film, *The Piano*, won the 1993 Palme D'Or at Cannes.

'THERE IS A SILENCE WHERE HATH BEEN NO SOUND
THERE IS A SILENCE WHERE NO SOUND MAY BE
IN THE COLD GRAVE, UNDER THE DEEP DEEP SEA.'

Thomas Hood (1799–1845)